WITHDRAWAL

Mathematical Proficiency for All Students

Toward a Strategic Research and Development Program in Mathematics Education

RAND Mathematics Study Panel
Deborah Loewenberg Ball, Chair

Prepared for the
Office of Educational Research and Improvement (OERI)
U.S. Department of Education

Science & Technology Policy Institute

RAND
EDUCATION

The research in this report was prepared for the Office of Educational Research and Improvement (OERI), U.S. Department of Education under Contract ENG-981273.

Library of Congress Cataloging-in-Publication Data

RAND Mathematics Study Panel.
    Mathematical proficiency for all students : toward a strategic research and development program in mathematics education / RAND Mathematics Study Panel, Deborah Loewenberg Ball, Chair.
       p. cm.
    "MR-1643."
    Includes bibliographical references.
    ISBN 0-8330-3331-X
    1. Mathematics—Study and teaching—United States. 2. Mathematics teachers—Training of—United States. I. Ball, Deborah Loewenberg, 1954–   . II. Title.

    QA13.R36 2003
    510' .71'073—dc21

                                                            2002155703

RAND is a nonprofit institution that helps improve policy and decisionmaking through research and analysis. RAND® is a registered trademark. RAND's publications do not necessarily reflect the opinions or policies of its research sponsors.

Cover design by Barbara Angell Caslon

© Copyright 2003 RAND

Published 2003 by RAND
1700 Main Street, P.O. Box 2138, Santa Monica, CA 90407-2138
1200 South Hayes Street, Arlington, VA 22202-5050
201 North Craig Street, Suite 202, Pittsburgh, PA 15213-1516
RAND URL: http://www.rand.org/
To order RAND documents or to obtain additional information, contact
Distribution Services: Telephone: (310) 451-7002; Fax: (310) 451-6915; Email:
order@rand.org

Developing proficiency in mathematics is an important goal for all school students. In light of current U.S. educational standards and the mathematics performance of U.S. students compared with the performance of students in other countries, a clear need exists for substantial improvement in mathematics achievement in the nation's schools. On average, U.S. students do not achieve high levels of mathematical proficiency, and serious gaps in achievement persist between white students and students of color and between middle-class students and students living in poverty.

To address these issues, the federal government and the nation's school systems have made and are continuing to make significant investments toward the improvement of mathematics education. However, the knowledge base upon which these efforts are founded is generally weak. Therefore, a strategic and coordinated program of research and development could contribute significantly to improving mathematics education in U.S. schools.

The RAND Mathematics Study Panel was convened as part of a broader effort to inform the U.S. Department of Education's Office of Educational Research and Improvement (OERI) on ways to improve the quality and relevance of mathematics education research and development. The 18 experts on the panel include education professionals, mathematicians, and researchers who have wide-ranging perspectives on the disciplines and methods of mathematics instruction. The panel was charged with drafting an agenda and guidelines for a proposed long-term strategic research and development program supporting the improvement of mathematics education. Such a program would inform both policy decisionmaking and the practice of teaching mathematics. This book presents the panel's recommendations for the substance and conduct of that proposed program. The panel's recommendations should be of interest to researchers who study mathematics instruction and to practitioners who teach mathematics.

This report is the second in a series of RAND reports on the topic of education research and development. The first report, *Reading for Understanding* (MR-1465-OERI, 2002), outlines a proposed research program aimed at reading comprehension education. Both reports should be of interest to individuals involved with education research and development programs in public or private agencies.

Funding for the RAND Mathematics Study Panel was provided under a contract with OERI. (Since this report was drafted, the U.S. Congress created the Institute of Education Sciences, which incorporates many OERI programs and functions.) The study was carried out under the auspices of RAND Education and the Science and Technology Policy Institute (S&TPI), a federally funded research and development center sponsored by the National Science Foundation and managed by RAND.

Inquiries regarding RAND Education or the S&TPI may be directed to the following individuals:

Helga Rippen, Director
Science and Technology Policy Institute
RAND, 1200 South Hayes Street
Arlington, VA 22202-5050
(703) 413-1100 x5351
Email: stpi@rand.org

Dominic Brewer, Director
RAND Education
RAND, 1700 Main Street
Santa Monica, CA 90407-2138
(310) 393-0411 x7515
Email: education@rand.org

CONTENTS

Preface iii

Figures ix

Summary xi

Acknowledgments xxv

RAND Mathematics Study Panel and RAND Staff xxvii

Chapter One
INTRODUCTION 1
Goals and Expectations 2
Challenges and Conflicts 3
Research Knowledge Needed to Meet Current Needs 4
A Program of Research and Development in Mathematics
    Education 5
Focus Areas of the Proposed Program . . . .
Program Goals 8
Foundational Issues 8
    Mathematical Proficiency 9
    Equity 10
Organization of This Report 12

Chapter Two
TEACHERS' MATHEMATICAL KNOWLEDGE: ITS
DEVELOPMENT AND USE IN TEACHING 15
Benefits of a Focus on Mathematical Resources for Teaching 16
What Do We Need to Know About Mathematical Knowledge for
    Teaching? 20
Developing a Better Understanding of the Mathematical
    Knowledge Needed for the Work of Teaching 23
Developing Improved Means for Making Mathematical
    Knowledge for Teaching Available to Teachers 24

Developing Valid and Reliable Measures of Knowledge for
      Teaching   25

Chapter Three
   TEACHING AND LEARNING MATHEMATICAL PRACTICES   29
   Mathematical Practices as a Key Element of Proficiency   30
   Benefits of a Focus on Mathematical Practices   33
   What Do We Need to Know About Learning and Teaching
      Mathematical Practices?   36

Chapter Four
   TEACHING AND LEARNING ALGEBRA IN KINDERGARTEN
   THROUGH 12TH GRADE   43
   Algebra as a Mathematical Domain and School Subject   44
   Benefits of a Focus on Algebra   47
   What Do We Need to Know About Teaching and Learning
      Algebra?   48
      Analyses and Comparison of Curriculum, Instruction, and
         Assessment   49
      Studies of Relationships Among Teaching, Instructional
         Materials, and Learning   50
   Impact of Policy Contexts on Student Learning   55

Chapter Five
   TOWARD A PARTNERSHIP BETWEEN GOVERNMENT AND
   THE MATHEMATICS EDUCATION RESEARCH COMMUNITY   59
   The Nature of the Proposed Program of Research and
      Development   59
   Criteria for the Quality of the Research and Development
      Program   62
   An Organizational Structure to Carry Out the Work   65
      Focus Area Panels   66
      Activities in Each Focus Area   67
      The Role of the Panel on Mathematics Education Research   67
   The Role of OERI in Conducting Practice-Centered Research and
      Development   68
      Leadership   68
      Managing for High Scientific Quality and Usefulness   69
      Concern for Enhancing the Research and Development
         Infrastructure   70
   Initial Steps in Implementing the Proposed Program   71
      Research Related to Standards of Proficiency to Be Achieved by
         Students   72

Research on the Nature of Current Mathematics Education in the
  Nation's Classrooms 73
Studies on the Development of Improved Measures of
  Mathematical Performance 75
Funding Resources 75
Chapter Six
  CONCLUSIONS.. 77
Bibliography 81

1.1. Cycle of Knowledge Production and Improvement of
Practice   6

5.1. Components of the Proposed Mathematics Education
Research and Development Program 62

5.2. Major Activities in the Proposed Mathematics Education
Research and Development Program 66

The teaching and learning of mathematics in U.S. schools is in urgent need of improvement. The nation needs a mathematically literate citizenry, but most Americans graduate from high school without adequate mathematical competence. In the 2000 National Assessment of Educational Progress, only 17 percent of grade-12 students nationally performed above a basic level of competence.[1] Furthermore, achievement gaps have persisted between white students and students of color, and between middle-class students and students living in poverty. As both a matter of national interest and a moral imperative, the overall level of mathematical proficiency must be raised, and the differences in proficiency among societal groups must be eliminated.

Improving proficiency in mathematics and eliminating the gaps in proficiency among social groups is and has been the goal of many public and private efforts over the past decade and a half. States and national professional organizations have developed standards for mathematics proficiency and assessments intended to measure the degree to which students attain such proficiency. Various programs have been developed to attract and retain more effective teachers of mathematics. New curricular materials have been developed along with training and coaching programs intended to provide teachers with the knowledge and skills needed to use those materials. However, these efforts have been supported by only a limited and uneven base of research and research-based development, which is part of the reason for the limited success of those efforts.

This report proposes a long-term, strategic program of research and development in mathematics education. The program would develop knowledge, materials, and programs to help educators achieve two goals: to raise the level of mathematical proficiency and to eliminate differences in levels of mathematical proficiency among students in different social, cultural, and ethnic groups. In the short term, the program is designed to produce knowledge that would sup-

---

[1]National Center for Education Statistics, 2001.

port efforts to improve the quality of mathematics teaching and learning with the teachers and materials that are now in place or that will become available over the next several years. More important, over 10 to 15 years, the program would build a solid base of knowledge for the design and development of effective instructional practice. That instructional practice, in turn, would enable the dual goals of increased levels of proficiency and equity in attaining proficiency to be achieved.

To yield maximum returns from the resources that are available for investment in mathematics education research and development, the program must focus on high-leverage areas of need; employ appropriate and valid methods for developing knowledge and practice; be grounded in and usable for instructional practice; develop and build on prior knowledge; and be coordinated, sustained, and cumulative. These program attributes will require sustained leadership from funders of mathematics education research and development—largely agencies of the federal government, including the U.S. Department of Education, the National Science Foundation, and the National Institutes of Health. Achieving these goals will also require that changes be made in the institutions of the research and development community and in those institutions' activities. In that regard, this report suggests both priorities for research and development activities and institutional arrangements intended to make the program outcomes rigorous, cumulative, and usable.

This report was commissioned by the Office of Education Research and Improvement (OERI, now the Institute of Education Sciences) as part of a larger RAND effort to suggest ways that education research and development could be made more rigorous, cumulative, and usable.[2] The RAND Mathematics Study Panel, which is composed of mathematics educators, mathematicians, psychologists, policymakers, and teachers, addresses the aforementioned concerns about the weak levels of mathematical proficiency of U.S. adults and students, and the inequities in the achievement of students from differing ethnic, cultural, and social groups. The work of the panel was inspired by the conviction that a program of research and development could be designed to help address these problems.

---

[2]This report was written before the reauthorization of the research program of the U.S. Department of Education. That reauthorization created an Institute for Educational Sciences (IES) within the department, replacing the OERI. We retained the designation OERI throughout this text. The features of the legislation authorizing the IES do not conflict with the proposals made here.

THE CONTEXT FOR A PRACTICE-CENTERED PROGRAM OF MATHEMATICS EDUCATION RESEARCH AND DEVELOPMENT

The mathematics performance of students and adults in the United States has never been regarded as wholly satisfactory. However, current goals and expectations for mathematics proficiency, as reflected in recent federal legislation such as the No Child Left Behind Act and numerous state policy initiatives, present a new and formidable challenge: Although the educational system has always produced some mathematically proficient individuals, now *every* student must be mathematically competent. The ambitious goal of mathematical proficiency for *all* students is unprecedented, and it places enormous demands on the U.S. educational system.

These new goals and expectations mean that skill in basic arithmetic is no longer a sufficient mathematics background for most adults. Although number sense and computational proficiency are important, other domains of mathematics knowledge and skill play an increasingly essential role in students' educational advancement and career opportunities. For example, the endless flood of quantitative information that people receive requires that they be familiar with statistics and have an understanding of probability. Algebra is vital as a medium for modeling problems, and it provides the tools for solving those problems. To reason capably about quantitative situations, students must understand and be able to use the basic principles of mathematical knowledge and mathematical practice that include, and go beyond, basic arithmetic.

While agreement on the broad goals for mathematics proficiency is widespread, the details of those goals and the means for achieving them are often the subject of disputes among educators, mathematicians, education researchers, and members of the public. These disputes center on the content that should be taught and how it should be taught. Arguments rage over curriculum materials, instructional approaches, and which aspects of the content to emphasize. Should students be taught "conventional" computational algorithms, or is there merit in exploring alternative methods and representations? When and how should calculators be used in instruction? What degree of fluency with mathematical procedures is necessary, and what sorts of conceptual understanding are important? What is the most appropriate approach to algebra in the school curriculum? Too often, questions such as these tend to reduce complex instructional issues to stark alternatives, rather than a range of solutions. More important, the intense debates over the past decade seem to be based more often on ideology than on evidence. In the view of the members of the RAND Mathematics Study Panel, the manner in which these debates have been conducted has hindered the improvement of mathematics education.

Amid this debate, U.S. schools are expected to provide more and better opportunities for students to learn mathematics. Yet, many schools lack the key resources needed to do so. For example, there is an acute shortage of qualified mathematics teachers,[3] and many widely used curriculum programs and assessment instruments are poorly matched with increasingly demanding instructional goals. While there is considerable policy-level pressure to seek "research-based" alternatives to existing programs and practices, the education and research communities lack rigorous evidence about the degree to which alternative existing or proposed curriculum and instructional practices effectively support all students' learning of mathematics.

Improving the effectiveness of school mathematics obviously depends on much more than research and development, but research and development are necessary if resources and energies are to be invested wisely. Future investments in the creation of mathematics education programs and materials, as well as investments in the training of teachers, require knowledge of the problems of instructional practice and the effectiveness of various approaches to addressing those problems.

However, despite more than a century of efforts to improve school mathematics in the United States, investments in research and development have been virtually nonexistent. Recent federal efforts to foster improvement in mathematics education are infrequently based on solid research, and federal funding for mathematics education research and development have been sporadic and uncoordinated. There has never been a long-range programmatic effort to fund research and development in mathematics education, nor has funding been organized to focus on knowledge that would be usable in practice.

This report is based on the premise that the production of knowledge about mathematics teaching and learning, and the improvement of practice based on such knowledge, depend on a coordinated cycle of research, development, implementation in practice, and evaluation, leading in turn to new research and new development. In the absence of such an effort, gaps in the knowledge base will continue to exist, and problems, particularly those associated with the equitable attainment of mathematical proficiency, will not be adequately addressed. Moreover, the success of such an effort requires that explicit attention be paid to the ways in which such knowledge can reach school classrooms in a form that teachers can use effectively to improve students' learning.

To guide such an effort, this report maps out a long-term agenda of programmatic research, design, and development in mathematics education. Rooted in

---

[3]National Commission on Mathematics and Science Teaching for the 21st Century, 2000.

practice in both its inspiration and its application, this program would coordinate efforts to create basic knowledge about the learning of mathematics through multiple forms of empirical inquiry. The program would tap the wisdom of practitioners, develop and test theories, and create and test interventions. If successful, such a program would produce resources supporting short-run improvements, and, over the course of 10 to 15 years, yield a strengthened base of knowledge useful for the sustained improvement of instructional practice. The proposed agenda must take into account the reality that public investments in research are a fraction of what is needed to deal with the scale and complexity of the problems. Therefore, difficult choices and careful designs will be required to gain maximum leverage and cumulative impact from available resources.

FOCUS AREAS FOR A LONG-TERM RESEARCH AND DEVELOPMENT PROGRAM

The limited resources that likely will be available for mathematics education research and development in the near future make it necessary to focus those resources on a limited number of topics. Because students' opportunities to develop mathematical proficiency are shaped within classrooms through their interaction with teachers and with specific content and materials, the proposed program addresses issues directly related to teaching and learning. We have selected three domains in which both proficiency and equity in proficiency present substantial challenges, and where past work would afford resources for some immediate progress:

1. Developing teachers' mathematical knowledge in ways that are directly useful for teaching

2. Teaching and learning skills used in mathematical thinking and problem solving

3. Teaching and learning of algebra from kindergarten through the 12th grade (K–12).

These are only the starting points for addressing mathematics proficiency problems. Fundamental problems to be addressed would remain and would be the subject of work in the longer-term collective effort we envision.

Developing Teachers' Mathematical Knowledge for Teaching

The first of the three focus areas in the proposed research and development program is *teachers' mathematical knowledge*. The quality of mathematics teaching and learning depends on what teachers *do* with their students, and what teachers *can do* depends on their knowledge of mathematics. Yet, numerous studies show that many teachers in the United States lack adequate knowledge of mathematics for teaching mathematics. Moreover, research indicates that higher proportions of classrooms in high-poverty areas, compared with classrooms in the nation as a whole, are staffed with poorly prepared teachers, which poses a particular problem from the perspective of the RAND panel's twin goals of mathematical proficiency and the equitable attainment of such proficiency.[4]

The knowledge base upon which to build policy and practice is poorly developed. While it is widely agreed among the mathematics education community that effective mathematics teaching depends on teachers' knowledge of content, the nature of the knowledge required for such teaching is poorly specified, and the evidence concerning the nature of the mathematical knowledge that is needed to improve instructional quality is surprisingly sparse. The same is true for the ways in which such teacher knowledge requirements for effective teaching may differ for diverse student populations. Building an improved understanding of these needs for mathematical knowledge, and developing effective means for enabling teachers to acquire and apply such understanding, would provide crucial help to the mathematics education community and to education policymakers. For these reasons, we propose a programmatic focus on three areas in which to frame fruitful lines of work on the knowledge needed for teaching:

1. Developing a better understanding of the mathematical knowledge needed for the actual work of teaching

2. Developing improved means for making useful and usable mathematical knowledge available to teachers

3. Developing valid and reliable measures of the mathematical knowledge of teachers.

To understand the mathematical knowledge needed for the work of teaching, the research community should investigate a number of key questions. The most central question addresses the role that teachers' knowledge of mathematics, their knowledge of students' mathematics, and their knowledge of students' out-of-school practices play in their instructional capabilities. Answers to this question must be developed in the context of specific mathematical domains. In addition, we feel it is important to develop a clearer delineation of the

---

[4]Council of Great City Schools, 2000; Darling-Hammond, 1994; National Commission on Teaching and America's Future, 1996.

knowledge and skills required of teachers to build students' capacity to engage in the kinds of mathematical thinking and mathematical problem solving that we term "mathematical practices."

In short, the purpose of this proposed area of work is to determine the specific knowledge of mathematical *topics and practices* that teachers need to teach particular domains of mathematics to specific students. This learning should ultimately be embodied in preservice programs, curricula, and materials supporting instruction, and professional development programs.

The professional development programs are the target of the second area of the proposed focus on teacher knowledge—developing improved means for making mathematical knowledge that is useful and usable for teaching available to teachers. The most fundamental effort in this area is identifying and shaping professional learning opportunities for teachers (or prospective teachers) to enable them to develop the requisite mathematical knowledge, skills, and dispositions to teach each of their students effectively. However, the challenge is not just to learn what is needed but to create arrangements for professional work that supports continued improvement of teachers' knowledge and their pedagogical skills. Meeting this challenge will involve experimenting with ways of organizing schools and school days to support these professional learning opportunities (e.g., scheduling of the week's classes, scheduling for collaborative planning and critiquing, freeing up time for mentoring, or providing on-demand professional development).

The advancement of professional practice in mathematics instruction can be supported through the development of "tools" that support teachers in their day-to-day work. Such tools include curriculum materials, technology, distance learning, and effective assessments. For example, teachers' manuals may provide teachers with opportunities to learn about mathematical ideas, about student learning of those ideas, and about ways to represent and teach those ideas. A recurring theme in our proposed program is the potential to make knowledge created through research and reflections on teaching practice usable by teachers by embodying that knowledge in tools, materials, and program designs.

The final component of the focus on teacher knowledge is the development of valid and reliable measures of mathematical knowledge for teaching. The lack of such measures has limited what one can learn empirically about what teachers need to know about mathematics and mathematics pedagogy. Similarly, the research community has lacked the tools to investigate how teachers' mathematical knowledge affects students' learning opportunities and their development of mathematical proficiency over time. As a result, the research and mathematics education communities lack evidence to mediate among the strongly held opinions about the mathematics knowledge that teachers need to have and how that knowledge can be gained and used effectively in teaching. The lack of valid and reliable measure of knowledge for teaching also inhibits the development of evidence-based policies related to teacher credentialing and teacher assignment to schools and classrooms.

Teaching and Learning Mathematical Practices

The second of the three focus areas in the proposed research and development program concerns the *teaching and learning of mathematical practices*. Mathematical practices involve more than what is normally thought of as mathematical knowledge. This area focuses on the mathematical know-how, beyond content knowledge, that constitutes expertise in learning and using mathematics. The term "practices" refers to the specific things that successful mathematics learners and users *do*. Justifying claims, using symbolic notation efficiently, defining terms precisely, and making generalizations are examples of mathematical practices. Another example of mathematical practices is the way in which skilled mathematics users are able to model a situation to make it easier to understand and to solve problems related to it. Those skilled individuals might use algebraic notation cleverly to simplify a complex set of relationships, or they might recognize that a geometric representation makes a problem almost transparent, whereas the algebraic formulation, although correct, obscures it.

Although competent use of mathematics depends on the ways in which people approach, think about, and work with mathematical tools and ideas, we hypothesize that these practices are often not systematically cultivated in school, although they may be picked up by students at home or in other venues outside of school. Moreover, it is likely that students with poorly developed mathematical practices will have difficulties learning mathematics. Thus, it is possible that part of the explanation for differences in students' mathematical proficiency is the degree to which they have had opportunities to develop an understanding of mathematics outside of school.

Thus, we propose a focus on understanding mathematical practices and how those practices are learned because we hypothesize that fostering competency in such practices could greatly enhance the education community's capacity to achieve significant gains in student proficiency in mathematics, especially among currently low-achieving students who may be the least likely to develop these practices in settings outside of school. Moreover, research work on these problems would also contribute to more-precise program goals and a more-precise definition of mathematical proficiency itself. These practices may also supply some of the crucial learning resources needed by teachers and students who are striving to meet increasingly demanding standards.

Significant research and development in mathematics education has already been conducted on processes such as problem solving, reasoning, proof, representation, and communication. Similarly, some researchers have investigated students' use of diagrams, graphs, and symbolic notation to lend meaning to and gain meaning about objects and their relationships to one another, while other researchers have probed students' approaches to proof.

Although past studies have investigated how students engage in particular practices, less is known about how these practices develop over time and how individual practices interact with one another. Little attention has been paid to the implications for the nature of the teaching required and the consequent requirements for teachers' own knowledge and practices in mathematics. To make progress based on past work, this focus area of our proposed research and development program would connect, organize, and expand upon those past studies under the umbrella of "mathematical practices" and address more systematically the question of how mathematical practices can be characterized, taught, and learned. In sum, this work in this focus area would do the following:

1. Develop a fuller understanding of specific mathematical practices, including how they interact and how they matter in different mathematical domains

2. Examine the use of these mathematical practices in different settings (e.g., practices that are used in various aspects of schooling, students' out-of-school practices, or practices employed by adults in their everyday and work lives)

3. Investigate ways in which these specific mathematical practices can be developed in classrooms and the role these practices play as a component of a teacher's mathematical resources.

TEACHING AND LEARNING ALGEBRA IN KINDERGARTEN THROUGH 12TH GRADE

A research and development program supporting the improvement of mathematical proficiency should focus on important content domains within the school mathematics curriculum. Coordinated studies of goals, instructional approaches, curricula, student learning, teachers' opportunities to learn, and policy signals—within a content domain—can be used to systematically investigate how various elements of instruction and instructional improvement affect student learning of that domain. We propose research and development related to the improvement of proficiency in algebra as the initial domain in which to work, and we have made it the third focus of the proposed program. "Algebra" is defined broadly here to include the mathematical ideas and tools that constitute this major branch of the discipline of mathematics, including classical topics and modern extensions of the subject.

We chose algebra as an appropriate initial mathematical domain for intensive focus for several reasons. One is that algebra is foundational in all areas of mathematics because it provides the tools (i.e., the language and structure) for representing and analyzing quantitative relationships, for modeling situations, for solving problems, and for stating and proving generalizations. These tools clearly are important for mathematically intensive professions. But algebraic notation, thinking, and concepts are also important in a number of workplace contexts and in the interpretation of information by Americans on a daily basis.

A second reason for selecting algebra lies in its gatekeeper role in kindergarten through 12th grade (K–12) schooling. Without proficiency in algebra, students cannot access a full range of educational and career options. Failure to learn algebra is widespread, and the consequences of this failure are that far too many students are disenfranchised. This curtailment of opportunity falls most directly on groups that are already disadvantaged and exacerbates existing inequities in our society.

Finally, many states now require students to demonstrate substantial proficiency in algebra in order to graduate from high school. These requirements are driven largely by statutory initiatives at both state and federal levels that are embodied, for example, in high-stakes accountability tests adopted by many states and in the federal No Child Left Behind legislation. This significant escalation of performance expectations in algebra creates challenges for students and teachers alike.

As a result of the enactment of new standards and a variety of mathematics education reform initiatives, the nation is in the midst of a major change in school algebra, including changes in views about who should take it, when they should learn it, what it should be about, and how it should be taught. As recently as ten years ago, the situation was relatively stable: Generally, algebra was studied by college-bound students, primarily those headed for careers in the sciences. Today, algebra is required of all students, and it is taught not only in high school but across all grades. A coordinated program of research and development could contribute evidence to mediate the debates surrounding the new policy moves. Moreover, the program could provide resources for the improvement of teaching and learning and for eliminating inequities in opportunities to become proficient in algebra.

Algebra is an area in which there has already been significant research. Since the 1970s, researchers in the United States and around the world have systematically studied questions about student learning in algebra and have accumulated useful knowledge about the thinking patterns, difficulties, and misunderstandings that students have in parts of this mathematics domain. This previous research work is invaluable as a foundation for what is needed now.

Despite the strong history of work in this area, we lack research about what is happening today in algebra classrooms; how innovations in algebra teaching and learning can be designed, implemented, and assessed; and how policy decisions shape student learning and affect equity. Because most studies have focused on algebra at the high school level, we lack knowledge about younger students' learning of algebraic ideas and skills. Little is known about what happens when algebra is viewed as a K–12 subject, what happens when it is integrated with other subjects, or what happens when it emphasizes a wider range of concepts and processes. Research could inform the perennial debates surrounding the algebra curriculum: what to include, emphasize, reduce, or omit. Three major components frame the recommended research agenda in algebra:

- Analyses and comparison of curriculum, instruction, and assessment

- Studies of relationships among teaching, instructional materials, and learning

- Studies of the impact of policy contexts on equity and student learning.

BUILDING THE INFRASTRUCTURE FOR A COORDINATED PROGRAM OF RESEARCH AND DEVELOPMENT

Our analysis of current issues related to mathematics education leads us to argue that achieving both mathematical proficiency and equity in the acquisition of mathematical proficiency should be fundamental goals for the nation. But mounting a program of research and development to support efforts to attain these goals will not be easy. It requires making judgments about where to focus efforts to build useful knowledge about mathematics education and to develop new designs for instruction and instructional improvement. The program will require workable means of gathering and deploying high-quality evidence to inform the debates on what constitutes effective instructional practice in school mathematics.

Because solutions to the problems we have identified are not the province of any single community of experts, it will be important to build a community of multidisciplinary professionals who have experience and expertise. Producing cumulative and usable knowledge will require the combined efforts of mathematicians, researchers, developers, practitioners, and funding agencies. This community must work together to size up the problems, set priorities, and plan useful programs of research. Thus, we believe the proposed program must also be conducted in such a way as to also increase the capacity of the mathematics education research and development community to carry out high-quality work.

Drawing on the work of the National Research Council and other groups, the RAND Mathematics Study Panel proposes several criteria to judge whether a mathematics research and development program is likely to meet high standards of rigor and usefulness. One set of criteria deals with the strategic framing, design, and conduct of relevant projects. A high-quality program of research and development should respond to pressing practical needs. It should build on existing research and be informed by relevant theory. Research methods should be appropriate to the investigation of a particular question and reflect the theoretical stance taken by the investigator. A coordinated program of research and development would also support groups of researchers to investigate significant questions from different theoretical and conceptual frames using methods consistent with both the questions and the frames.

A second set of criteria concerns the kinds of communication, information sharing, and critiquing that are vital to building high-quality knowledge and evidence-based resources for practice. To support syntheses of results, replication of results, and generalization of results to other settings, researchers and developers must make their findings public and available for critique through broad dissemination to appropriate research, development, and practice communities. The chains of reasoning that lead from evidence to inference should be made explicit so that claims can be inspected. Publicizing claims and evidence will make it possible to compare and synthesize findings, methods, and results from various projects. This comparison and synthesis can help support a dynamic exchange between researchers and developers, leading to better designs coupled with better evidence of the consequences of using those designs.

A research and development program meeting these criteria will require a significant design and management effort. The funders of mathematics education research and development must play the central role in this effort, but they should perform that role in collaboration with both the research and development and the mathematics education communities. We envision an approach that would coordinate research, development, and expertise resources to build the systematic knowledge necessary for making mathematical proficiency an attainable goal for all students. Reaching these goals requires the establishment of a research infrastructure to develop the capacity for such work, and that infrastructure, in turn, requires the following:

- Active overall leadership for the design and organization of the program

- Management of the process of solicitation and selection of projects in a way that promotes work of high scientific quality and usefulness

- Deliberate development of individual, institutional, and collective capacity within the field.

In this report, we present a possible organizational structure to meet these requirements. The organization would consist of an overarching group, the Mathematics Education Research Panel, comprising a wide range of individual expertise and interests, which would advise the OERI on possible directions for the program. From time to time, this panel would assess the progress of the program as a whole, synthesize the program's results, and suggest any new initiatives that are needed. In addition, we propose the formation of three subpanels who would provide planning and guidance for each of the three focus areas of the program—mathematical knowledge for teaching, mathematical practices, and algebra. The membership of these subpanels should represent a wide range of viewpoints and include mathematics education researchers, mathematicians, mathematics educators, cognitive scientists, developers and engineers, experts in measurement, and policymakers. The subpanels would play an active and continuing role in advising OERI on the management of the focus area programs.

A cornerstone of good research and development program management is an effective process for supporting and maintaining the quality of the work that is funded. We recommend the creation of a peer review system that involves individuals with high levels of expertise in relevant subjects and research methods. We believe such a system will be most effective if it is separate from the research planning, synthesis, and advisory functions that we have proposed for the panels. A peer review system that has the confidence of the field (and of the scientific community in general) is likely to attract high-quality researchers and provide reasonable assurance that quality proposals are supported.

Investment in infrastructure will contribute significantly to the quality of the program. Key infrastructure elements include the development of common measures that can be used to gather evidence across projects and deliberate nurturing of new scholars and developers. Modes of communication and opportunities for communication among and between researchers and practitioners should be developed and supported. High-quality work depends on open debate unconstrained by orthodoxies and political agendas. It is crucial that the composition of the panels and the extended research communities be inclusive, engaging individuals with a wide range of views and skills.

CONCLUSIONS

Mathematics education is an area of vital national interest, but it is also a subject of considerable controversy. Claims and counterclaims abound concerning the value of distinctive curricular strategies and specific curricula, requirements for teacher knowledge, and standards that students should meet. For the most part, these debates are poorly informed because research evidence is lacking. The program we propose in this report is most likely to gain the necessary political support if it begins with activities intended to reshape these debates into empirically based investigations of the issues that underlie important competing claims. Thus, we recommend that work be initially supported in three key areas:

1. Studies providing evidence to inform the necessarily political decisions concerning standards of mathematical proficiency to be met by students

2. Studies of current instructional practice and curriculum in U.S. classrooms

3. Studies that collect and adapt existing measures of mathematical performance or develop new ones that can be used across studies in the proposed program.

While such initial investigations would necessarily be broad, they can contribute to understanding in the three proposed focus areas and lay the foundation for an improved relationship between research and practice and more enlightened public discourse.

The program we describe is both ambitious and strategic. Shaped by hypotheses about what will yield payoffs in increased mathematical proficiency for all students, it is a program that will have high scientific rigor and an emphasis on the usability of the knowledge that it produces. The program will involve unprecedented scrutiny, testing, and revision of instructional interventions, building evidence on how those interventions work and what it takes to make them effective.

ACKNOWLEDGMENTS

The RAND Mathematics Study Panel and its members are grateful to the many groups and individuals who played a role in shaping this report.

First, the panel is indebted to the independent peer reviewers who critiqued our initial draft: Jere Brophy, Michigan University; Douglas Carnine, University of Oregon, together with R. James Milgram, Stanford University; Jere Confrey, University of Texas at Austin; Cindy Chapman, Inez Elementary School, New Mexico; Paul Cobb, Peabody College, Vanderbilt University; Sue Eddins, Illinois Mathematics Science Academy; Daniel Goroff, Harvard University; Glenda Lappan, Michigan State University; Judith Sowder, San Diego State University; Alan Schoenfeld, University of California Berkeley; and David G. Wright, Brigham Young University. Their reviews contributed significantly to reshaping the original draft.

The panel also thanks the various professional associations and the persons within them who, by individual or group response, provided valuable commentary on the RAND Mathematics Study Panel's initial draft that was posted on the project Web site (www.rand.org/multi/achievementforall/math/). Individual practitioners and scholars, too numerous to list by name, independently sent us helpful comments and suggestions on the draft report; we thank each and every one of them for taking the time to review and offer thoughtful comments on the report's initial draft.

At RAND, we have many people we wish to thank. Gina Schuyler Ikemoto, Elaine Newton, Kathryn Markham, and Donna Boykin provided guidance and support that facilitated our work; Nancy DelFavero, editor of the final report, dedicated numerous hours to carefully reading the text and making improvements in the prose. Tom Glennan devoted endless time to this project, offering invaluable reactions, advice, and skilled insight, as well as careful writing. Others also played crucial roles: Fritz Mosher contributed in numerous essential ways to the panel's deliberations and to the construction of the report itself. Mark Hoover of the University of Michigan read critically, searched out references, and helped with ideas. We are grateful to Carole Lacampagne of the Office of Educational Research and Improvement, U.S. Department of Education, who served as lead staff on this project while in residence at RAND and devoted steady oversight, organization, and counsel.

From OERI, Kent McGuire gave direction and inspiration to the panel's original charge. Mark Constas and Valerie Renya provided thoughtful oversight of our activities and Grover (Russ) Whitehurst contributed valuable reviews and advice on earlier drafts.

The final report has been significantly improved by the contributions. In the end, however, it was the work of the panel who, with Tom Glennan and Fritz Mosher's counsel and support, produced and developed the ideas and proposals outlined in the report. In a time when we hear so often about bitter conflicts among the different groups who have a stake in mathematics education, the RAND Mathematics Study Panel was successful at working collaboratively and in deliberately soliciting and using criticism from diverse critical readers and reviewers. The panel's success provides evidence that the differences in perspective and experience can be essential resources in the effort to improve mathematics education. We hope that our efforts will contribute to an ongoing discussion aimed at developing, over time, a high-quality and productive research and development enterprise.

Deborah Loewenberg Ball, Chair
RAND Mathematics Study Panel

RAND MATHEMATICS STUDY PANEL AND RAND STAFF

STUDY PANEL

Deborah Loewenberg Ball, Chair, University of Michigan

Hyman Bass, University of Michigan

Jo Boaler, Stanford University

Thomas Carpenter, University of Wisconsin–Madison

Phil Daro, New Standards, University of California

Joan Ferrini-Mundy, Michigan State University

Ramesh Gangolli, University of Washington

Rochelle Gutiérrez, University of Illinois

Roger Howe, Yale University

Jeremy Kilpatrick, University of Georgia

Karen King, Michigan State University

James Lewis, University of Nebraska

Kevin Miller, University of Illinois

Marjorie Petit, The National Center for the Improvement
of Educational Assessment

Andrew Porter, University of Wisconsin–Madison

Mark Saul, Bronxville High School

Geoffrey Saxe, University of California–Berkeley

Edward Silver, University of Michigan

STAFF

Thomas Glennan, Senior Advisor for Education Policy

Gina Schuyler Ikemoto, Education Research Analyst

Carole Lacampagne, Senior Researcher, Mathematics

Frederic Mosher, Senior Researcher

Chapter One

INTRODUCTION

The United States needs to substantially improve the teaching and learning of mathematics in American schools. A growing number of Americans believe not only that the future well-being of our nation depends on a mathematically literate population but also that most adults are weak in mathematics, with some groups disproportionately worse off. The basic level of mathematical proficiency needs to be raised substantially, and the gaps in proficiency across societal groups need to be eliminated.

Despite years spent in mathematics classes learning about fractions, decimals, and percents, many well-educated adults, for example, would respond incorrectly to the following question:

> If the average salaries of a particular group within a population are 16 percent less than the average salary of the entire population, and one wants to give the individuals in that group a raise to bring them up to parity, what should the raise be—16 percent, something more, or something less?[1]

Although they may have been taught the relevant calculation skills, what most American adults remember from school mathematics are rules that are not grounded in understanding. Many adults would be unable to answer this problem correctly or even to attempt to reason through it. Proficiency in formulating and solving even relatively simple percent problems is not widespread.

In the past, mathematical proficiency was regarded as being important primarily for those headed for scientific or mathematical professions. But times have

---

[1]Although 16 percent may seem to be the obvious answer, it is not correct. For example, if the average salary is $40,000, then the salaries of the underpaid group are 16 percent of $40,000 ($6,400) less than the average salary—i.e., $33,600. If one had assumed that 16 percent of the lower salary was the required raise, the raise would have amounted to only $5,376 ($33,600 x 0.16)—clearly, not enough to make up the $6,400 difference between the higher and lower salaries. Instead, one needs to determine what percentage of $33,600 equals $6,400. A simple calculation ($40,000 divided by $33,600) reveals that $40,000 is approximately 19 percent more than $33,600, so the raise required to bring the lower salaries up to par with the higher ones would be a bit more than 19 percent.

changed. Today, broad agreement exists that mathematical proficiency on a wide scale matters. That few people might be able to solve problems like the one on the previous page is troubling because American adults will require substantial mathematical proficiency to participate fully and productively in society and the economy of the 21st century.

While the mathematics performance of the U.S. population has never been seen as satisfactory, today dissatisfaction with that performance has become intense, and it is growing. Over the past decade or so, we have witnessed a movement to raise educational standards, and we have seen persistent efforts to increase educators' accountability for achievement. The recent legislation entitled "No Child Left Behind" has committed the nation to ensuring that all children meet high standards of mathematical proficiency.[2] The consequences will be enormous if states, school districts, and schools fail to make rapid and continuous progress toward meeting those standards over the next decade.

The American educational system has always been able to develop mathematical proficiency in a small fraction of the population, but current policies create goals and expectations that present a dramatic new challenge: Every student now needs competency in mathematics. This goal of achieving mathematical proficiency for all students is unprecedented, and it places vastly more ambitious performance demands on all aspects of the educational system.

In this report, commissioned by the Office of Education Research and Improvement (now the Institute for Educational Sciences [IES]), we argue that a focused, strategic program of research and development in mathematics education can make a meaningful and essential contribution to achieving America's goals for school mathematics.[3]

GOALS AND EXPECTATIONS

The aims of teaching mathematics in school are rooted in the basic justifications for public education. One element is social: A responsible and informed citizenship in a modern economic democracy depends on quantitative understanding and the ability to reason mathematically. Such knowledge is important in making judgments on public issues and policies of a technical nature. A second element is personal: Mathematics extends the options available in one's

---

[2]*No Child Left Behind Act of 2001,* 2002.

[3]This report was written before the reauthorization of the research program of the U.S. Department of Education. That reauthorization created an IES within the department, replacing the Office of Educational Research and Improvement (OERI). We retained the designation OERI throughout this text. The features of the legislation authorizing the IES do not conflict with the proposals made here.

career as well as in one's daily life. People's opportunities and choices are shaped by whether they know and are able to use mathematics. A third element is cultural: Mathematics constitutes one of humanity's most ancient and noble intellectual traditions. It is an enabling discipline for all of science and technology, providing powerful tools for analytical thought and the concepts and language for creating precise quantitative descriptions of the world. Even the most elementary mathematics involves knowledge and reasoning of extraordinary subtlety and beauty.

Economic considerations are also relevant to the goals of school mathematics: In today's economy, with its emphasis on high technology, most jobs that support a decent standard of living demand strong and flexible quantitative skills. As workplaces evolve, the mathematical ideas that students need on the job will change, and people must be prepared to learn, analyze, and use mathematical ideas they have never encountered in school or used before.

CHALLENGES AND CONFLICTS

Current goals for mathematics proficiency and the accompanying higher expectations that go with them have complicated the task of improving school mathematics. We no longer assume that facility in paper-and-pencil arithmetic is the only mathematics that most adults will ever need. Other domains of mathematics—algebra, in particular—have become increasingly essential to educational advancement and career opportunities. We also do not assume that students can become proficient in mathematics only if they enter school equipped with some special innate abilities and predisposition for math proficiency. Students can be taught strategies and techniques to compensate for their limited experiences outside of school and their inadequate preparation in mathematics. Although comparisons with the mathematics performance of students in other countries demonstrate that U.S. students' performance is inadequate, those comparisons also suggest that this performance could be much greater if we made specific improvements in our curriculum, teaching, and assessment practices.

Further complicating the process of improving school mathematics are disputes about what content should be taught and how it should be taught.[4] Some observers argue that mathematics should be taught primarily by teachers providing clear, organized expositions of concepts and procedures and then giving students opportunities to practice those procedures and apply those concepts. Others contend that teachers should design ways to engage students firsthand in exploring the meaning of mathematical procedures, rather than simply

---

[4]See, for example, Loveless, 2001.

showing them how to carry them out. Yet others want students to memorize procedures and develop skills so that understanding can follow from those activities. And others want to put understanding first and foremost, contending that in the computer age, a heavy emphasis on procedural skill is no longer relevant. Arguments also rage over the nature of school mathematics: Should it be mostly abstract and formal or mostly concrete and practical? With these basic issues in play, battles have been waged over curriculum materials. The intense debates that filled the past decade have often impeded much-needed collective work on improvement. Moreover, they have been based more often on ideology than on evidence.

Amid this conflict, U.S. schools are expected to provide more and better opportunities for students to learn mathematics and to do so despite chronic shortages of resources. Most school districts lack a cadre of qualified, mathematically proficient teachers,[5] and it is not clear whether widely used curriculum programs and assessment instruments are adequate for the task of helping schools meet new and more demanding instructional goals. Schools are seeking information on the effectiveness of curriculum materials and instructional practices to help them make better decisions about how to support all children's learning of mathematics. More and more, the public is insisting that the choices the schools make be "research based."

RESEARCH KNOWLEDGE NEEDED TO MEET CURRENT NEEDS

Tackling the problems of school mathematics obviously depends on much more than research, but research is necessary if human energies and other resources are to be invested wisely. Future investments require knowledge about problems of instructional practice and about ways to address those problems. Where such knowledge exists and has been appropriately used, it has paid off.

Examples of research that has made a difference in school mathematics practices include studies of how teachers can use knowledge of students' arithmetic strategies to develop their problem-solving and computational skills,[6] studies of characteristics of professional development that enhance teachers' instruction and their students' learning,[7] and studies of how to improve mathematics instruction in urban schools.[8] But research-based knowledge about mathematics education has often been of little use to teachers. It often does not address

---

[5]National Commission on Mathematics and Science Teaching for the 21st Century, 2000.

[6]Carpenter et al., 1989; Carpenter, Fennema & Franke, 1996; Cobb, Wood & Yackel, 1991; Hiebert et al., 1997; Kilpatrick, Swafford & Findell, 2001.

[7]Borko & Putnam, 1996; Cohen & Hill, 2000; Saxe, Gearhart & Seltzer, 1999.

[8]Garet et al., 2001; Silver & Lane, 1995; Silver & Stein, 1996.

problems that concern teachers, for instance, or it is communicated in ways that make it seem esoteric and render its implications unclear or impractical.

Despite more than a century of efforts to improve school mathematics in the United States, efforts that have yielded numerous research studies and development projects, investments in research and development have been inadequate. Federal agencies (primarily the National Science Foundation and the U.S. Department of Education) have contributed funding for many of these efforts. But the investments have been relatively small, and the support has been fragmented and uncoordinated. There has never been a long-range programmatic effort devoted solely to funding research in mathematics education, nor has research (as opposed to development) funding been organized to focus on knowledge that would be usable in practice. Consequently, major gaps exist in the knowledge base and in knowledge-based development.[9]

The absence of cumulative, well-developed knowledge about the practice of teaching mathematics and the limited links between research and practice have been major impediments to creating a system of school mathematics that works. These impediments matter now more than ever. The challenge faced by school mathematics educators in the United States today—to achieve both mathematical proficiency and equity in the attainment of that proficiency—demands the development of new knowledge and practices that are rooted in systematic, coordinated, and cumulative research.

A PROGRAM OF RESEARCH AND DEVELOPMENT IN MATHEMATICS EDUCATION

To build the resources needed to meet the new challenges outlined above, this report maps out a long-term, strategic program of research and development in mathematics education that connects theory and practice. If successful, the program would produce resources to support mathematics teaching and learning in the near term. After 10 to 15 years, it would have built a solid base of knowledge needed for sustained improvement in effective instructional practice. The proposed agenda for the program must take into account the reality that public investments in research are a fraction of those needed given the scale and complexity of the problems. The proportion of the national education budget spent on research and development is far below the levels of research and development spending in most sectors of the economy. Hence, difficult choices and careful designs will be required to gain maximum leverage and cumulative impact from available resources. In every aspect of the research and development program, attention to the dual themes of mathematical profi-

---

[9]Wilson, Floden & Ferrini-Mundy, 2001.

ciency and equity is vital, a requirement demanding the development and testing of instruments to assess how well various groups of students are progressing on the road toward proficiency.

We view the production of knowledge and the improvement of practice as being a cycle of research, development, improved knowledge and practice, and evaluation, leading in turn to new research, new development, and so on. This implies that problems can be initially addressed and worked on at different points in that cycle, as shown in Figure 1.1.

A coordinated program of research and development should be designed to strengthen relations among these efforts so that investments in one would contribute to the others. The evolving knowledge base builds on what is being tried in practice, and what is developed for practice draws on new insights from research. Individual projects might work at one or more points in the cycle. No single project by itself would be expected to yield a definitive answer to any significant problem. Instead, program leaders would coordinate a varied progression of projects—interventions, research, and studies of various kinds—in ways that build knowledge and practice. One corollary of this approach is that interventions, whose primary goal is the improvement of practice, could also have, by design, a concomitant goal of testing theoretical ideas and generating new theoretical insights and research questions.

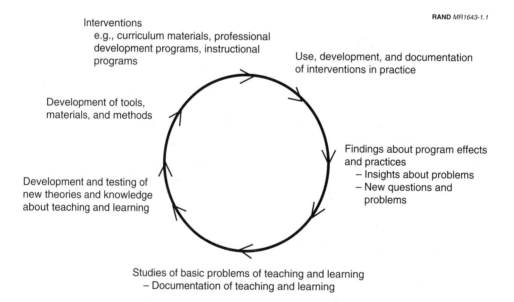

Figure 1.1—Cycle of Knowledge Production and Improvement of Practice

The program should be designed as a joint undertaking involving cooperation among researchers, practitioners, developers, and funders. This requires coordinated funding. But cooperation and coordination does not mean that all work would be guided by some rigid program design. Nevertheless, projects would be linked in a system that coordinates different kinds of work, from survey research and descriptive work, to basic inquiry, to small-scale developments, to efforts to develop and use programs or approaches across contexts.

For a cooperative undertaking such as this to be successful requires direct investments of not just money but also time and imaginative thinking. Significant responsibility for the design of the effort must lie with the sources of funding of the work and the management authority that resides in that function. Among the challenges the funders face are creating ways to commission work that stimulate the field's imagination and initiative, and creating institutional structures that can engage the communities of research and practice in taking collective and disciplined responsibility for this work. A proposal for those structures is outlined in Chapter Five.

FOCUS AREAS OF THE PROPOSED PROGRAM

The overarching goal of the proposed research and development program is to achieve mathematical proficiency for all students. Because students' opportunities to develop mathematical proficiency are shaped within classrooms through interaction with teachers and interaction with specific content and materials, the program must address issues directly related to teaching and learning. In selecting specific areas for a research and development focus, we sought to identify areas in which the goals of both greater mathematics proficiency for all students and greater equity in the levels of proficiency attained by students from differing backgrounds present substantial challenges requiring a long-term collective effort. We also sought to identify areas of research and development in which past research would provide a basis for some immediate progress. In outlining a proposed program, we focused on three areas (which are discussed in greater depth in Chapters Two through Four):

1. Developing teachers' mathematical knowledge in ways directly useful for teaching

2. Teaching and learning skills for mathematical thinking and problem solving

3. Teaching and learning of algebra from kindergarten through 12th grade (K–12).

Our aim is to map out a coordinated agenda of research and development that, by the end of a decade and a half, would provide the nation with the knowledge, materials, and programs needed to make the overarching goal of mathematical proficiency and equity attainable.

PROGRAM GOALS

The first goal of the proposed research and development program is to address the critical problems surrounding the teaching and learning of mathematics in the United States. Our proposals are based on the RAND Mathematics Study Panel's hypotheses about where and how investments in research and development will yield the greatest opportunities for improving American mathematics education. Rooted in practice in both its inspiration and its application, this program seeks to coordinate and combine theory building, multiple forms of empirical inquiry, interventions, and the wisdom of experience. Research-based knowledge should be justified in ways that help to warrant its intended use, and the problems that research addresses should be derived from the problems and goals of practice. We do not intend to neglect basic research in this endeavor, but we argue that what is often understood as "basic research" would be enhanced by more considered attention to its relationship to the activities of students and teachers.

Because solutions to the problems of mathematics education require multiple types of expertise, a second goal is to build a multidisciplinary professional community of people who have experience and expertise in practice, research, development, and policy. This community would work together to size up problems, set priorities, and plan useful programs of research and development. The work of the RAND Mathematics Study Panel represents one such effort to bring together some of the diverse groups of people who have a stake in the improvement of mathematics education: scholars from various disciplines, practitioners, developers, and policymakers. Reaching these aims will require the creation of an infrastructure for research and development to build the capacity for such work.

Although we are optimistic that the proposed program is both appropriate and promising, we recognize that implementing the results of the program in the schools will raise significant policy issues. We do not attempt to delineate these policy issues in any detail, but in several places in this report we do make observations about the possible need for policy research.

FOUNDATIONAL ISSUES

Underlying the proposed mathematics research and development program are two foundational issues: proficiency and equity. Not only must the overall level of student proficiency be raised, but also differences in proficiency should no longer be associated with race, social class, gender, language, culture, or ethnicity. We see these as challenging but compatible goals.

Mathematical Proficiency

The notion of mathematical proficiency that we use in this report is based on a conception of what it means to be competent in mathematics.[10] This concept is represented by five separate but intertwined strands:

- Conceptual understanding—comprehension of mathematical concepts, operations, and relations

- Procedural fluency—skill in carrying out procedures flexibly, accurately, efficiently, and appropriately

- Strategic competence—ability to formulate, represent, and solve mathematical problems

- Adaptive reasoning—capacity for logical thought, reflection, explanation, and justification

- Productive disposition—habitual inclination to see mathematics as sensible, useful, and worthwhile, coupled with a belief in the value of diligence and in one's own efficacy.

These strands of proficiency are interconnected and coordinated in skilled mathematical reasoning and problem solving. Arguments that pit one strand against another—e.g., conceptual understanding versus procedural fluency—misconstrue the nature of mathematical proficiency. Because the five strands are interdependent, the question is not which ones are most critical but rather when and how they are interactively engaged. The core issue is one of balance and completeness, which suggests that school mathematics requires approaches that address all of the strands. Mathematical proficiency is more complex than the simplistic or extreme positions in current debates over curriculum recognize.

Because mathematical proficiency is a foundation of this research and development program, it is central to each of the areas proposed for intensive, programmatic focus. A major part of the knowledge teachers need for teaching relates to mathematical proficiency and how it can be developed in their students. If teachers hold a restricted view of proficiency and are not themselves proficient in mathematics as well as in teaching, they cannot bring their students very far toward current goals for school mathematics. Thus, addressing

---

[10]Kilpatrick, Swafford & Findell, 2001.

the development and use of teacher knowledge is the first critical priority of the proposed research and development program. A second critical priority, if teachers are to help all students attain mathematical proficiency, is the identification, analysis, and development of mathematical practices. In fact, our conception of practices can be seen as another way of framing important aspects of these strands of proficiency. Third, by making algebra a subject matter focus of this program, we are calling for coordinated research and development to probe the nature of mathematical proficiency in a major area of mathematics and to investigate what is necessary to develop it.

Although we regard the above conception of mathematical proficiency as being foundational, we also recognize that it needs further specification. A research program focused on proficiency must work toward a clearer articulation of what the strands of mathematical proficiency mean and how they relate to each other and interact over the course of a student's learning of mathematics. The program also must foster the development of measures or assessments that better capture these conceptions of proficiency and how proficiency grows over time. And the program should work to provide evidence of how performance on these measures relates to the ability of students and adults to function effectively in other aspects of their lives. Such research would help the policy and practice communities develop a better understanding of what proficiency is and what the standards for proficiency should be. This knowledge would provide a stronger basis for making wise decisions about how to improve mathematics education in this country.

Equity

Defining the goal of mathematics education as providing everyone with the opportunity to gain mathematical proficiency brings the issue of equity front and center. The harsh reality is that our educational system produces starkly uneven outcomes. Although some students develop mathematical proficiency in school, most do not. And those who do not have disproportionately been children of poverty, students of color, English-language learners, and, until recently, girls.[11] Recent National Assessment of Educational Progress (NAEP) results show that the gaps in mathematics achievement by social class and ethnicity have not diminished over the years.[12] In 2000, over 34 percent of white students in grade 8 attained either "proficient" or "advanced" performance on the NAEP, up from 19 percent in 1990. Among African-American students, results were dismal, with the percentage holding steady at 5 percent. And

[11]Abt Associates, 1993; Kenney & Silver, 1997; Orland, 1994; Silver & Kenney, 2000.

[12]Braswell et al., 2001; Silver & Kenney, 2000.

although the percentage of Hispanic students who attained "proficient" or "advanced" status more than doubled, the result was still low, at 9 percent.

Lack of success in mathematics has significant consequences: Algebra, for example, plays a significant gatekeeping role in determining who will have access to college and certain career opportunities. The "gates" tend to be closed to the less advantaged, either by default—when the schools they attend simply do not offer advanced mathematics courses—or by discrimination—when low expectations for student performance lead to educational tracking that differentiates among students and therefore further limits students' opportunities to develop math proficiency.

The three areas on which we focus in this study were chosen largely because they directly relate to the issue of equity:

- First, we focus on the mathematical knowledge needed for teaching because there is no more strategic point at which to address inequity in opportunities to learn mathematics. Schools in the highest-poverty, most ethnically diverse areas of the United States tend to have teaching forces with the poorest preparation in mathematics.[13] Paying teachers more and tapping new pools of potential teaching talent are important, but those measures will not help less-advantaged students as long as their teachers lack the understanding of mathematics needed to engage, inspire, and educate these students. We need to understand exactly what mathematical knowledge is needed for teaching, especially for teaching diverse groups of students, and we need to understand how that knowledge is learned and used together with knowledge of students (their backgrounds, existing skills, interests, and such) and pedagogy. Some studies suggest the importance of teachers being able to understand the use of mathematics in the everyday lives of their students and to use that understanding in their lessons. But just how important these things are, and what way they are important, are empirical questions and, therefore, are vital issues to be addressed in a research and development program addressing inequity in mathematics instruction.

- Our second focus explores mathematical practices: the mathematical activities in which mathematically proficient people engage as they structure and accomplish mathematical tasks. This focus on practices calls attention to aspects of mathematical proficiency that are often left implicit in instruction, going beyond specific knowledge and skills to include the habits, tools, dispositions, and routines that support competent mathematical activity.

---

[13]Council of Great City Schools, 2000; Darling-Hammond, 1994; National Commission on Teaching and America's Future, 1996.

Owing at least in part to differing opportunities across societal groups to learn these mathematical practices, skill in these practices is unequally distributed in the population and therefore need to be addressed in school. Yet, far too often, mathematics instruction in less-advantaged schools remains a matter of simply drill and practice rather than also trying to initiate students into mathematical practices—learning what it means to create, understand, do, use, and enjoy mathematics.[14] The inclusion of this focus in the proposed program is based on our hypothesis that a fuller understanding of this implicit dimension of proficiency, and the corresponding development of support for teachers in making mathematical practices a specific component of classroom instruction, could lead to major advances in closing the performance gap between various groups.

• Third, we focus on algebra as a strategic content area in the program we envision for many reasons, some of which are cognitive, some of which are disciplinary, and others more social and cultural. But a key reason for this focus is the role that algebra plays in controlling access to further education and good jobs. The reasons for algebra's gatekeeper role are both disciplinary and historical. First, algebra functions as a language system to express ideas about quantity and space, and therefore serves as a foundation, as well as prerequisite, for all branches of the mathematics discipline. Second, algebra has come to play a prominent role in the organization of schooling, school subjects, and curriculum in the United States, within and beyond mathematics. Its role as a gatekeeper has divided students into classes with significantly different opportunities to learn. Currently, disproportionately high numbers of students of color and students living in poverty are not adequately prepared in algebra and do not have access to serious mathematics beyond this level.[15] A close look at the issue of equity in the teaching and learning of algebra will provide valuable specifics for understanding and dealing with inequities in this preparation.

ORGANIZATION OF THIS REPORT

In Chapters Two through Four, we discuss the three proposed focus areas for investments in research and development: developing teachers' mathematical knowledge and the use of that knowledge in teaching (Chapter Two), the teaching and learning of mathematical practices (Chapter Three), and the teaching and learning of algebra throughout grades K–12 (Chapter Four). Each area directly supports the proposed program's goals of building knowledge for

---

[14]Anyon, 1981; Haberman, 1991.

[15]Payne & Biddle, 1999.

improved practice aimed at developing mathematical proficiency across the country's population of school children. In those chapters, we show how the proposed program is strategically designed to mobilize existing resources and to build on previous research in the area to make substantial progress in the short term and to achieve fundamental changes in the quality of mathematics education in the long term. In Chapter Five, we begin by presenting the elements of the proposed program, and then outline the criteria for a strategic program that is built on existing research and linked to relevant theory, and end with the initial steps in creating the program. Chapter Six summarizes our conclusions and recommendations.

Chapter Two

TEACHERS' MATHEMATICAL KNOWLEDGE:
ITS DEVELOPMENT AND USE IN TEACHING

Our proposed research agenda centers on building the resources needed for high-quality mathematics instruction. Given that the quality of instruction depends fundamentally on what teachers *do* with students to develop their mathematical proficiency, and given that what teachers *can do* depends fundamentally on their knowledge of mathematics, we recommend that the first of the three strands of research in the proposed program focus on the mathematical knowledge required for teaching mathematics and on the key resources needed to use that knowledge in teaching. In particular, this strand of research would focus on the materials and institutional contexts that support the deployment of mathematical knowledge in teaching.

Thus, if the program is well managed, its results could have a profound effect on the professional education of mathematics teachers and on various components of the education system, such as certification requirements, teacher assessments, and teachers' guides. Such an effect would require coordination of work across a variety of studies and interventions. Our decision to focus on knowledge of mathematics for teaching furthers the overarching goal of the work of the RAND Mathematics Study Panel: achieving mathematical proficiency for all students. We need better insight into the ways in which teachers' mathematical knowledge, skills, and sensibilities become tools for addressing inequalities in students' opportunities to learn. What role does teachers' mathematical knowledge play in their being able to see the potential mathematical merit in students' spontaneous ideas and strategies for solving mathematics problems? What role does this knowledge play in enabling teachers to connect the mathematics in students' everyday world with school mathematics? How does teachers' knowledge of students' mathematical thinking and students' personal interests combine with teachers' knowledge of mathematical content to shape their presentation and representation of that content, use of materials, and ability to understand their students?

BENEFITS OF A FOCUS ON MATHEMATICAL RESOURCES FOR TEACHING

Our focus on mathematical resources for teaching both extends an existing body of mathematics education research and development and targets important practical problems. Over the past several decades, two refrains have echoed throughout the discourse on teachers' knowledge of mathematics: (1) the mathematical knowledge of U.S. teachers is weak, and (2) the mathematical knowledge needed to enable effective teaching is different from that needed by mathematicians. But efforts to improve our understanding of the mathematical knowledge needed for teaching have lacked an adequate theoretical and empirical basis to guide the connection of mathematical knowledge with the work that teachers need to do.

This lack of a theoretical and empirical basis has created impediments to improvement in the training and development of teachers. Since the late 1980s, new programs, materials, curricular frameworks, standards, and assessments have been developed, all aimed at improving mathematics education. Still, teachers are the crucial element in the learning of mathematics. Teachers require substantial mathematical insight and skill to use new curriculum materials that emphasize understanding as well as skill, open their classrooms to wider mathematical participation by students, make responsible accommodations for students with varying prior knowledge of mathematics, and help more students to succeed on more-challenging assessments.

In light of these requirements, many efforts have been undertaken to help teachers develop a more robust mathematical understanding to support their teaching: Courses and workshops offer teachers opportunities to revisit and relearn the mathematical content of the school curriculum, states have raised the content-knowledge requirements for teacher certification, and programs have been developed to attract mathematically experienced and skilled people into teaching. However, these programs lack theoretical foundations and adequate evidence of their effectiveness. Despite some successful efforts to develop teachers' mathematical knowledge through professional development, teachers participating in those efforts are often no better able to understand their students' ideas, to ask strategic questions, or to analyze the mathematical tasks contained in their textbooks than they were before these efforts.[1]

The need for knowledge of mathematical content seems obvious. Who can imagine teachers being able to explain methods for finding equivalent fractions, answer student's questions on why $n^0 = 1$, or represent place value without un-

---

[1]See, for example, Borko, Eisenhart & Brown, 1992; Lubinski et al., 1998; Thompson & Thompson, 1994, 1996; and Wilcox et al., 1992.

derstanding the mathematical content? Less obvious, perhaps, is the nature of the knowledge of mathematical content needed for *effective teaching*: What do teachers need to know of mathematics in order to teach it? What are the mathematical questions and problems that teachers face in their daily work? What is involved in *using* mathematical knowledge in the context of teaching? What does it take for teachers to use mathematical knowledge effectively as they make instructional decisions and instructional moves with particular students in specific settings, especially with students who traditionally have not performed well in mathematics?

In 1985, Lee Shulman and colleagues introduced the term "pedagogical content knowledge" to the teaching and teacher education research lexicon.[2] This term called attention to a special kind of teacher knowledge that links content, students, and pedagogy. In addition to general pedagogical knowledge and content knowledge, Shulman and his students argued,[3] teachers need to know things like what topics children find interesting or difficult and the representations of mathematical content most useful for teaching a specific content idea.[4] This notion of pedagogical content knowledge not only underscored the importance of understanding subject matter for teaching, but it also made plain that ordinary adult knowledge of a subject could often be inadequate for teaching that subject.

Existing investigations of teacher knowledge have painted a large and distressing portrait of teachers' mathematical knowledge. In the late 1980s, researchers at the National Center for Research on Teacher Education developed new and better methods of assessing teacher content knowledge. One new technique was to pose questions in the context of teaching. In this way, the interviews probed how well respondents were able to use their mathematics knowledge for the work teachers have to do—for example, deciding if a student's solution is mathematically valid, spotting an error in a textbook, or posing problems well.

When researchers began to look closely at these issues, their analyses revealed how thin most teachers' understanding of mathematics and mathematics pedagogy are. Both elementary and secondary teachers, whether they entered teaching through traditional or alternative routes, appeared to have some sound mechanical knowledge as indicated by the fact that they were often, although not always, able to solve straightforward, simple problems. When asked to explain their reasoning, however, or why the algorithms that they used worked, neither elementary nor secondary teachers displayed much under-

---

[2]Shulman, 1986.

[3]Wilson, Shulman & Richert 1987.

[4]Shulman, 1986, 1987.

standing of the concepts behind their answers. Secondary teachers who had majored in mathematics were, for example, unable to explain why division by zero was undefined or to connect the concept of *slope* to other important mathematical ideas. Other researchers, using the same instruments or similar ones, found similar results.[5] Although teachers participating in these studies often— but surprisingly inconsistently— got the "right answers," they lacked an understanding of the meanings of the computational procedures or of the solutions. Their knowledge was often fragmented, and they did not integrate ideas that could have been connected (e.g., whole-number division, fractions, decimals, or division in algebraic expressions).

These findings are not surprising, given that most teachers have learned mathematics within the same system that so many are seeking to improve. The fact that their understanding is more rule-bound than conceptual, and more fragmented than connected, reflects the nature of the teaching and curriculum that they, like other American adults, experienced in elementary and secondary schools. However, if teachers are to lead the improvement of mathematics teaching and learning, it is crucial that they have opportunities to revise and develop their own mathematical knowledge. To accomplish this, program developers and educators need better insight into the nature of the mathematics used for the work of teaching.

We also need better insight into the ways that materials and institutional contexts can either assist or impede teachers' efforts to use mathematical knowledge as they teach. For example, how can teachers' guides be crafted to provide opportunities for teachers to learn mathematics? How can they be designed such that teachers understand the mathematical purposes pertinent to an instructional goal? How can those guides be designed to help teachers use their mathematical knowledge as they prepare lessons, make sense of students' mistakes, and assess students' contributions in a class discussion? Mentoring, team teaching, lesson study, and other organizational structures provide further opportunities for developing and helping teachers to convey mathematical knowledge, but we have little systematic knowledge concerning the effects of such resources.[6]

Recently, Liping Ma's work[7] has added to our understanding of knowledge of mathematics for teaching and the resources that support its use by proposing an important idea that she calls "profound understanding of fundamental

---

[5]See, for example, Eisenhart, Borko, & Underhill, 1993; Even, 1990; Simon, 1993; Ma, 1999; Wheeler & Feghali, 1993; and Graeber & Tirosh, 1991.

[6]Gutiérrez, 1996.

[7]Ma, 1999.

mathematics." Ma describes the "knowledge packages" that were evident in the knowledge of the 72 Chinese elementary teachers she interviewed. These knowledge packages represented a refined sense of the organization and development of a set of related ideas in a particular arithmetic domain. The Chinese teachers articulated ideas about "the longitudinal process of opening up and cultivating [a set of ideas] in students' minds."[8] Their knowledge packages consisted of key ideas that "weigh more" than other ideas in the package, sequences for developing the ideas, and "concept knots" that link crucially related ideas. Moreover, the development and use of the knowledge packages is supported by institutional practices of mentoring and socialization, as well as professional collaboration.

Ma's notion of "knowledge packages" is a particularly generative form of pedagogical content knowledge. Central to her ideas of how to make mathematical knowledge usable in teaching is the ability to structure relationships among a set of ideas and to map out the longitudinal trajectories along which ideas can be effectively developed.

In sum, research over the past several decades has clearly indicated that the knowledge of mathematics needed to be an effective teacher is different from the knowledge needed to be a competent professional mathematician or the knowledge that is needed to use mathematics in some other field such as engineering or science. At the same time, research has provided evidence that many teachers of mathematics lack sufficient mathematical knowledge to teach mathematics effectively. Research also suggests that even well-developed materials when used by teachers who neither understand the content or the difficulties that students typically experience in learning that content do not by themselves lead to the development of student proficiency.

Although we know that teaching requires special knowledge of mathematics, we lack robust empirical descriptions of the mathematical knowledge associated with successful teaching. We also lack persuasive theory upon which to base the design of effective programs for teachers' learning. We turn now to the issue of what we need to know to design such programs or experiences.

WHAT DO WE NEED TO KNOW ABOUT MATHEMATICAL KNOWLEDGE FOR TEACHING?

Although common sense suggests that the best preparation for teaching K–12 mathematics might be an undergraduate degree in mathematics, the real answer is not that simple. First, most elementary school teachers are responsible

---

[8]Ma, 1999, p. 114.

for teaching all subjects, not simply mathematics, and so they cannot major in any single field as undergraduates. Instead, they typically take a few college mathematics courses in a mathematics department. Second, the mathematics of the K–12 curriculum does not map well onto the curriculum of an undergraduate mathematics degree. Even if prospective teachers majored in mathematics as undergraduates, the last time they may have studied the mathematics of the K–12 curriculum was when they were K–12 students themselves. Thus, although it is often overlooked, the problem of developing mathematical knowledge for teaching is important for the preparation and professional learning of secondary as well as elementary and middle school teachers.[9]

Therefore, one area that we have targeted for programmatic work concerns the content-specific knowledge used for teaching mathematics and how and where the use of such knowledge makes a difference for high-quality instruction. In the past decade, numerous studies have probed teachers' knowledge of mathematics in a few key areas, and the findings so far have been sobering. Division has garnered enormous attention, followed by fractions, rational numbers, and multiplication.[10] Moreover, many other key mathematical areas and ideas warrant attention—discrete mathematics, number systems, integers, geometry, place value, probability, algebra—to name a few. We know little about what teachers need to understand specifically within these areas. We do not know much about how teachers need to be able to get inside mathematical ideas to make them accessible to students. And we do not know what they need to know of the mathematics that lies ahead of them in the curriculum. We need studies that would help us learn about the mathematical resources needed to teach mathematics effectively.

Research on teachers' mathematical knowledge has frequently focused on substantive knowledge—or *topics*. As Kennedy points out,[11]

> Because the main goal of [current] reformers is to instill a deeper understanding in students of the central ideas and issues in various subjects and to enable students to see how these ideas connect to, and can be applied in, real-world situations, it therefore makes sense to require that teachers themselves also understand the central ideas of their subjects, see these relationships, and so forth.

To a lesser extent, past research has also probed teachers' knowledge and use of *mathematical thinking and problem solving* (what we termed *mathematical practices* in Chapter One) as a component of mathematical knowledge. Why

---

[9]See Conference Board of the Mathematical Sciences (2001) for a thorough examination of and recommendations for the mathematical preparation of teachers at all levels.

[10]See, for example, Post et al., 1991, and Simon & Blume, 1994a, 1994b, 1996.

[11]Kennedy, 1997.

does this component matter? As students learn mathematics, they are engaged in using and doing mathematics, as are their teachers. They represent ideas, develop and use definitions, interpret and introduce notation, figure out whether a solution is valid or not, and recognize patterns. Students and teachers together are constantly engaged in situations in which mathematical practices are essential. Inevitable as this is, teachers and curricula vary enormously in the explicit attention they give to this component of mathematical knowledge. Conceptions of teacher knowledge have seldom considered the kinds of mathematical practices that are central to teaching. For example, rarely do teachers have opportunities to learn about notions of definitions, generalization, or mathematical reasoning.

The use of knowledge, whether of content or of mathematical practices, is an important subject for research. What are strategic ways to conceptualize the work of teaching that are theoretically and empirically based and will effectively guide efforts to improve teaching and learning? What aspects of the work of teaching depend on knowledge of mathematics? For instance, one important set of activities in teaching is identifying, interpreting, and responding to students' mathematical ideas, difficulties, and ways of thinking. Several researchers have profitably mined this domain of teaching.[12] Research in this area needs to be extended to examine what it takes for teachers to hear, understand, and work effectively with the widest possible range of students in mathematics education and to identify other important aspects of teachers' instructional work where mathematical knowledge for teaching is crucial.

Other "resources" can contribute to the quality of mathematics instruction. Recent studies of how people use mathematics outside of school reveal that candy sellers, basketball players, and shoppers, for example, all use mathematics in their everyday lives.[13] However, little work exists on how knowledge of such uses might be effectively used in mathematics classrooms. Such understanding seems likely to have considerable importance to achieving greater equity in the acquisition of proficiency in mathematics.

We know that students bring knowledge from outside of school to the mathematics classroom, and that such knowledge can differ significantly by race and by class.[14] Can information about students' out-of-school practices be recognized and used by teachers so that they can connect mathematical content to students in more meaningful ways? How might such information be used to en-

---

[12]Barnett, 1991, Barnett et al., 1994; Carpenter, Fennema, & Franke, 1996; Schifter, 1998.

[13]See, for example, Saxe, 1991; Saxe, Gearhart, & Seltzer, 1999; Lave, 1988; Nunes, Schliemann, & Carraher, 1993; Nasir, 2000, 2002; and Civil, 2002.

[14]McNair, 2000.

gage students who traditionally do not perform well in mathematics? Although some professional development efforts emphasize ways in which teachers can build on students' out-of-school practices (e.g., riding the subway) and prepare teachers to help students translate everyday activities into abstract mathematical equations,[15] much remains to be done to extend this line of work in ways that would make it usable for classroom instruction.

Still other research has investigated the role teachers' beliefs and expectations about different kinds of students play in their teaching.[16] Much of this work explores how teachers' knowledge and expectations about students affect students' opportunities to learn as well as their learning. A teachers' ability to see and make good use of their students' mathematical efforts depends in large measure on whether he or she can see and make sense of the mathematics in those efforts. Research suggests that teachers' expectations for their students' performance often shape their assumptions about the correctness or merit of a particular student's work. A teacher whose mathematical knowledge is thin is less likely to recognize the mathematical sense in a student's representation or solution, leading to an inappropriate assessment of the student's capabilities. But, while much has been learned, more remains to be uncovered about how such expectations and beliefs play out for particular topics or mathematical practices.

Although significant progress has been made toward better understanding the mathematical knowledge needed for teaching, we need to know more if we are to improve teachers' mathematical preparation. We identify three areas around which to frame and focus a fruitful line of work on knowledge for teaching: (1) developing a better understanding of the knowledge of mathematics needed in practice for the actual work of teaching; (2) developing improved ways to make useful and usable knowledge of mathematics available to teachers; and (3) developing valid and reliable measures of the mathematical knowledge for teaching.

Developing a Better Understanding of the Mathematical Knowledge Needed for the Work of Teaching

One line of work would extend current research on mathematical knowledge needed for teaching to other mathematical topics and to the realm of mathematical practices and their role in teaching. Another line of work would explore

---

[15]Moses & Cobb, 2001.

[16]See, for example, work by scholars such as Aguirre, 2002; Atweh, Bleicher, & Cooper, 1998; Gutiérrez, 1996; Reyes, Capella-Santana, & Khisty, 1998; and Rosebery & Warren, 2001.

the relationship of this knowledge to the instructional contexts in which it is used. In this effort, some important questions need to be answered:

- What specific knowledge of mathematical *topics and practices* is needed for teaching particular areas of mathematics to particular students?

- What mathematical thinking and problem-solving practices are important in the work of teaching? How and where should such practices be developed in the course of teaching? What do teachers need to know about such practices to be able to support students' engagement in and learning of such practices?

- What knowledge and expectations about students' mathematical thinking and capabilities are needed for teaching specific mathematics and mathematics practices to particular students?

- How does or should students' existing content-specific knowledge shape teachers' decisions about the presentation and representation of content, the use of materials, and the ability to hear and understand their students in particular areas of mathematical content?

- What role does teachers' knowledge of mathematics, knowledge of students' mathematics, and knowledge of students' out-of-school practices play in a teacher's ability to address inequalities in students' opportunities to learn?

- What mathematical and student-oriented sensibilities are needed to enable teachers to use their knowledge effectively in practice?

Many opportunities for research are made possible by the adoption of different curricula across the nation. Do the new curriculum series demand more, or different, mathematical knowledge than the textbooks that have more traditionally been used in classrooms? How do different sorts of teachers' guides affect what teachers are prepared to do, and can do, with their students? While studies focused on such curricula would contribute to an understanding of the implementation challenges in the curricula themselves, *collectively* such studies could add much to the body of understanding about teachers' knowledge of mathematics that we have argued is needed.

Developing Improved Means for Making Mathematical Knowledge for Teaching Available to Teachers

A second line of proposed work in this focus area concerns the construction of systems and institutional practices that can make mathematical knowledge for teaching more systematically available. Although we have argued that evidence exists that mathematical knowledge can make a significant impact on instruction, making that knowledge usable and using it in practice remains an important part of the problem to be solved.

We have identified three classes of research and development opportunities. One approach to supporting the effective use of mathematical knowledge in practice focuses on teachers' professional learning opportunities. A second lies in the arrangements for professional work that would support both learning and the use of what is learned. The third class centers on the design of useful tools to support mathematically knowledgeable practice. Issues important to this research and development include:

- **Professional learning opportunities:** What learning opportunities enable teachers to develop the mathematical knowledge, skills, and dispositions needed for teaching? How can teachers be helped to develop the requisite mathematical knowledge, skills, and dispositions in ways that enable them to teach each of their students effectively? What learning opportunities promote teachers' *use* of such mathematical knowledge and skills and their ability to act on such dispositions?

- **Arrangements for professional work:** Over the past decade, many efforts have been made to organize the professional work of teachers to allow them to better develop their mathematics knowledge. Although different approaches have their advocates, we do not know about the relative effectiveness of those approaches in different contexts. For example, arrangements for organizing professional practice that permit some teachers to specialize in mathematics and others to focus on instruction in other content areas could be investigated. Another possibility is to organize teachers' grade-level assignments in ways that facilitate collaboration in learning from teaching. Do organizational arrangements that allow teachers to move through grades together with their students afford the development of mathematical knowledge that is difficult to attain when teachers remain at the same grade level from year to year? Alternatively, does collaboration on lessons with others teaching at the same level and using the same materials develop and facilitate the use of mathematical knowledge (e.g., teachers engaged in practices of "lesson study" similar to those widely used in Japan). This class of work could both systematically examine existing arrangements for professional work and be used to design and test new ones.

- **Tools to support mathematically knowledgeable practice:** What are the characteristics of tools that support the effective use of mathematical knowledge in teaching? Such tools might include curriculum materials, technology, distance learning, and assessments. For example, a wide variety of new curriculum materials have been designed with substantially enhanced teachers' manuals. These manuals are intended to provide teachers with opportunities to learn about mathematical ideas, about student learning of these ideas, and about ways to represent and teach these ideas. Some research shows that teachers' use of teachers' guides are shaped by their work conditions—for example, whether they have time for planning—as well as their knowledge of mathematics. How might such materials be designed and used more effectively by teachers, and with what effect on practice?

Widespread curriculum development and new textbook adoptions provide opportunities to design systematic investigations to uncover how various forms of professional development—with different structures, content, and pedagogical approaches—interact with new text adoptions to affect the quality of instruction. For example, a school district that adopts a new curriculum series could offer three distinct forms of professional support for the development of teachers' usable knowledge and skill. This would provide the opportunity to compare the effects on teachers' capacity to use curricula skillfully and their students' learning from those curricula within the same environment.

Developing Valid and Reliable Measures of Knowledge for Teaching

A third element of this agenda centers on the need for reliable and valid measures of the content knowledge required in teaching. Such measures are needed for certifying teachers, designing and assessing professional training programs, and the redesign of programs for preservice preparation of teachers. On the whole, existing measures are weak.

Typical approaches to measuring content knowledge include using a major or minor in mathematics or mathematics courses that were taken as proxy measures of teachers' mathematics knowledge. For example, some researchers have investigated the relationship between a major in mathematics and gains in student achievement. Several studies found a (slight) positive correlation between teachers' majors in a subject matter and gains in student achievement,[17] but in another study, researchers found a "ceiling effect"—that is, increases in student achievement were positively correlated with teachers' courses in mathematics up to about five courses, after which the benefits of taking more mathematics courses appeared to be negligible.[18] To complicate matters further, other studies have found some positive correlations between mathematics-specific edu-

---

[17]Ferguson, 1991.
[18]Monk, 1994.

cation course work and student achievement, but not between mathematics courses and student achievement.[19]

A major problem with proximate measures for teachers' knowledge—such as undergraduate degrees or number of courses taken—is that they are poor indicators of what teachers actually know and how they use that knowledge in teaching. Complicating things further is the variation in what constitutes a "major" across institutions of higher education (e.g., at some colleges and universities, one does not have a "major" but rather fulfills a "concentration"). This variability makes it difficult to know exactly what teachers have had the opportunity to learn in their master's program or undergraduate courses. In recent years, researchers have developed protocols for probing teachers' mathematics knowledge more directly. They have developed interview protocols, written assessments, and observational instruments. These tools have proved useful for learning what teachers know and how they think, and, in some cases, how they reason about a situation in teaching mathematics, analyze a student's response, evaluate a student's work, or make judgments about goals for future instruction. Although some of these instruments have been shared across research projects, few have been tested or validated.

The lack of sophisticated, robust, valid, and reliable measures of teachers' knowledge has limited what we can learn empirically about what teachers need to know about mathematics and mathematics pedagogy. The lack of measures also limits our understanding about how such knowledge affects the learning opportunities of particular students and their development of mathematical proficiency over time.

To identify the mathematical knowledge needed in teaching, and to study the impact of various kinds of learning opportunities, the field needs reliable and valid measures of teachers' knowledge and of their use of such knowledge in teaching. A range of tools is needed, including survey measures, performance tasks, and written and interactive problems. This line of work should build on the past 15 years of work on teacher assessment.[20] Such measures would permit teacher knowledge to be investigated as a variable in virtually all studies of mathematics teaching.

Questions worth pursuing in this area include the following:

---

[19]Begle, 1979; Monk, 1994.

[20]For example, Shulman and colleagues at Stanford University with the Teacher Assessment Project (1985–1990); National Board for Professional Teaching Standards; Interstate New Teacher Assessment and Support Consortium; The Praxis Series developed by Educational Testing Service; the National Center for Research on Teacher Education and the Teacher Education and Learning to Teach study at Michigan State University (1986–1991); and the Study of Instructional Improvement currently under way at the University of Michigan.

- Building on previous studies of the knowledge used in effective instruction, what are the domains in which to measure teachers' knowledge? How can those domains be sampled? How homogeneous or topic-specific is teachers' knowledge of mathematics?

- How should reliable measures of teachers' mathematical knowledge be developed, piloted, and validated?

- What assessment tools are needed to carry out research on how teachers' knowledge of mathematics interacts with their other knowledge, such as their knowledge of particular students, and how it shapes their instruction?

- Would specific measurement instruments enable us to better understand how various sorts of professional development affect teachers' usable content knowledge and their ability to use that content knowledge in particular settings?

- How can research on models of instruction and their effects on student learning be enhanced by the use of the measures of mathematical knowledge discussed in this chapter?

Chapter Three

TEACHING AND LEARNING MATHEMATICAL PRACTICES

Because expertise in mathematics, like expertise in any field, involves more than just possessing certain kinds of knowledge, we recommend that the second strand of the proposed research and development program focus explicitly on mathematical know-how—what successful mathematicians and mathematics users *do*. We refer to the things that they do as *mathematical practices*. Being able to justify mathematical claims, use symbolic notation efficiently, and make mathematical generalizations are examples of mathematical practices. Such practices are important in both learning and doing mathematics, and the lack of them can hamper the development of mathematics proficiency.

Our rationale for this focus is grounded in our fundamental concerns for mathematical proficiency and its equitable attainment. While some students develop mathematical knowledge and skill, many do not, and those who do acquire mathematical knowledge are often unable to use that knowledge proficiently.[1] Further, debates over the improvement of students' mathematics achievement are often intertwined with questions about what we mean by "proficiency." The work related to mathematical practices that the RAND Mathematics Study Panel proposes should contribute to a better understanding of proficiency and hence to greater clarity and consensus about goals for the improvement of mathematical education.

It is important to note that this focus is the most speculative of the three we propose in this report. After much deliberation, we chose it because we hypothesize that a focus on understanding these practices and how they are learned could greatly enhance our capacity to create significant gains in student achievement, especially among currently low-achieving students who may have had fewer opportunities to develop these practices. Our belief that this focus would contribute to greater precision about what is meant by mathematical proficiency reinforced our decision to make it a priority.

---

[1]Boaler, 2002, and Whitehead, 1962.

MATHEMATICAL PRACTICES AS A KEY ELEMENT OF PROFICIENCY

Our choice of the term "practices" for the things that proficient users of mathematics do is rooted in a definition given by Scribner and Cole:

> By a *practice* we mean a recurrent, goal-directed sequence of activities using a particular technology and particular systems of knowledge. We use the term "skills" to refer to the coordinated sets of actions involved in applying this knowledge in particular settings. A practice, then, consists of three components: technology, knowledge, and skills. We can apply this concept to spheres of activity that are predominantly conceptual (for example, the practice of law) as well as to those that are predominantly sensory-motor (for example, the practice of weaving). All practices involve interrelated tasks that share common tools, knowledge base, and skills. But we may construe them more or less broadly to refer to entire domains of activity around a common object (for example, law) or to more specific endeavors within such domains (cross-examination or legal research).[2]

Those of us in the RAND study panel believe that too little attention has been paid to research on the notion of practice as set forth by Scribner and Cole. When considering what it means to *know* mathematics, most people think of one's knowledge of topic areas, concepts, and procedures. Of course, these things are central to knowing mathematics. But mathematics is a domain in which what one does to frame and solve problems also matters a great deal. Simply "knowing" concepts does not equip one to use mathematics effectively because using mathematics involves performing a series of skillful activities, depending on the problem being addressed.

Because the concept of "mathematical practices" will be unfamiliar to many readers, we begin by illustrating what is involved in this concept. We chose an example that involves elementary school students because we want our readers to see that what we are discussing here is important to learning and using mathematics at any grade level. In this example, a third-grade class is dealing with an unexpected claim made by one of the children concerning even and odd numbers.

As you read this example, you may become puzzled, or even impatient. You may be asking, why doesn't the teacher immediately set the student straight by clarifying the definitions of even and odd numbers? Try instead to look for the mathematical practices that students are using and learning to use. Notice, too, that no choice needs be made on the part of the teacher between the mastery of content and the development of practice. The students are developing and using certain mathematical practices at the same time that their understanding of

---

[2]Scribner & Cole, 1981.

the definitions of even and odd numbers are strengthened and made more explicit. By the end of this classroom episode, the students know what determines whether a number is even or odd. In addition, the practices in which they engage will be important for many other mathematical problems, puzzles, and confusing situations that they will face in the future.

Near the beginning of a class, one of the boys in the class volunteers something that he says has occurred to him. He has been thinking that the number 6 "could be even or it could be odd." Of course, this is wrong—6 is even. His classmates object. The teacher does not immediately correct the child, but instead lets the other students respond. She recognizes that figuring out how to resolve this debate might offer students an important opportunity to learn how to deal with confusion about core mathematical concepts.

Using the number line above the chalkboard, one girl tries to show the student that his theory creates a problem because if 6 is odd, then 0 would be odd, too. She is relying on her knowledge that the even and odd numbers alternate on the number line. Unconvinced, the boy persists. To show why he thinks that 6 can be thought of as odd as well as even, he draws six circles on the board, divided into three groups of two circles, as such:

"There can be three of something to make six, and three is *odd*," he explains. Many hands go up as the other students disagree with this logic. "That doesn't mean that 6 is odd," replies one classmate. Another classmate uses the definition of even numbers to show that 6 has to be even because you can divide 6 into two equal groups and not break anything in half. Finally, another girl, after pondering further what the first student is saying, asks him why he doesn't also say that 10 is "an even number and an odd number" since it is composed of *five* groups of two, and 5 is odd. She makes a drawing just like his, except with five groups of two circles. When he agrees that 10 could also, like 6, be odd, the classroom erupts with objections, and another girl explains firmly that "it is not according to how many groups it is." She explains that the definition of an even number means that what is important is whether a number can be grouped by twos "with none left over." Using the first student's drawing, she shows that the key point is that no circles are left over.

Over the next few minutes, the children spend time clarifying definitions for even and odd numbers, and they also have a bit of mathematical fun noticing that other even numbers have the property that the first student observed—14 is seven groups of two, 18 is nine groups of two, and so on. Several children contribute examples excitedly, and finally one girl observes that there seems to be a pattern in such numbers—the numbers with this quality of "oddness" appear to be the alternating even numbers.

At first glance, the children in the previous example might seem to be merely helping a classmate who is confused about a simple fact—whether 6 is even or odd—or who is unaware that the definitions of even and odd are mutually exclusive. A closer look at the situation, however, shows that the students are using and learning some important mathematical *practices* that actually enable them to resolve the confusion—i.e., no one ends up believing that 6 can be both even and odd—and they also explore some significant mathematical ideas along the way. For example, several of the children use representations to communicate mathematical ideas—one student uses the number line and another creates a diagram, which is then used by the other children. One student makes a mathematical claim, which is seen as a matter of common concern by the others who deploy their shared knowledge to illustrate the contradictions that are implicit in the claim. If 6 can be odd, another student reasons, then 0 might also be odd. And another student generalizes the first student's reasoning about the number 6, arguing that the first student must have to accept that 10 could also be odd.

Attentive to the importance of language in resolving this problem, the students refer to and use various definitions of even and odd numbers to make and support their arguments. They also seek to compare alternative definitions of even and odd numbers. Further generalizing the first student's argument about the "oddness" of 6, they identify a class of even numbers having the same characteristic—the numbers can be grouped into odd multiples of two—and notice patterns in this class of numbers.

These activities—mathematical representation, attentive use of mathematical language and definitions, articulated and reasoned claims, rationally negotiated disagreement, generalizing ideas, and recognizing patterns—are examples of what we mean by *mathematical practices*. As the mathematician Andrew Wiles endeavored to prove Fermat's last theorem, he engaged in similar practices—representation, reconciliation, generalization, and pattern-seeking—that enabled him to make one of the world's greatest mathematical breakthroughs, as detailed in a number of biographies depicting the famous proof.[3] These practices and others are essential for anyone learning and doing mathematics proficiently.

Competent learning and use of mathematics—whether in the context of algebraic, geometric, arithmetic, or probabilistic questions or problems—depend on the way in which people approach, think about, and work with mathematical tools and ideas. Further, we hypothesize that these practices are not, for the most part, explicitly addressed in schools. Hence, whether people somehow ac-

_____

[3]Singh, 1997.

quire these practices is part of what differentiates those who are successful with mathematics from those who are not. Our proposed research and development program would help to answer key questions in this area, such as: How are these practices learned? What role do they play in the development of proficiency? How does the lack of facility with such practices hamper the learning of mathematics? And what affects their equitable acquisition?

BENEFITS OF A FOCUS ON MATHEMATICAL PRACTICES

Significant research has been conducted on mathematical practices such as problem solving, reasoning, proof, representation, and communication. The ways in which students approach and solve problems of various kinds, the processes used by expert problem solvers, and the heuristics that function to guide the solving of problems all have attracted the attention of researchers, and we know a lot in these areas.[4] For example, some researchers have investigated students' use of diagrams, graphs, and symbolic notation to lend and gain meaning about objects and their relationships with one another.[5] Others have probed students' knowledge of proof.[6] This research has illuminated the importance of these processes in a student's approach to learning and using mathematics. However, many important questions about mathematical practices remain unanswered, and the lack of adequate knowledge about these practices has led to controversy over mathematics education improvement efforts.

New curricula and standards have paid more attention to processes such as problem solving and justifying. However, weak implementation of instruction intended to build facility with these processes has led to contentious debates among educators, mathematicians, and members of the public over whether these curricula and standards are "watering down" mathematics instruction. To build a consensus on what should be taught, and to improve teaching and learning, we need a greater understanding of what it takes to learn and teach mathematical reasoning, representation, and communication in ways that contribute to mathematical proficiency. We hypothesize that people who do well with mathematics tend to have developed a set of well-coordinated mathematical practices and engage in them flexibly and skillfully, whereas those who

---

[4]See, for example, Charles & Silver, 1989; Goldin & McClintock, 1984; National Council of Teachers of Mathematics, 1989, 2000; Ponte et al., 1991; Schoenfeld, 1985, 1992; and Vershaffel, Greer, & De Corte, 2000.

[5]See, for example, DiSessa et al., 1991; Even, 1998; Goldin, 1998; Janvier, 1987; Kaput, 1998a; Leinhardt, Zaslavsky & Stein, 1990; Noss, Healy, & Hoyles, 1997; Owens & Clements, 1998; Vergnaud, 1998; and Wilensky, 1991.

[6]See, for example, Balacheff, 1988; Bell, 1976; Blum & Kirsch, 1991; Chazan, 1993; Coe & Ruthven, 1994; De Villiers, 1990; Dreyfus & Hadas, 1996; Hanna & Jahnke, 1996; Maher & Martino, 1996; and Simon & Blume, 1996.

are less proficient have not. We also suspect that such practices play an important role in a teacher's capacity to effectively teach. If we are correct, investing in understanding these "process" dimensions of mathematics could have a high payoff for improving the ability of the nation's schools to help all students develop mathematical proficiency.

A key reason for focusing on practices for learning, doing, and using mathematics is to confront the pervasive—and damaging—cultural belief that only some people have what it takes to learn mathematics. Along the lines of the groundbreaking work that Carol Lee[7] and her colleagues are doing in English literature, which is focused on literary interpretation and on connecting students' prior skills and interests with their evolving literary practices, this focus could enable a serious challenge to the pervasive inequalities seen in school mathematics outcomes. In their work, Lee and her colleagues approach the problem from two directions. On one hand, they seek to uncover and articulate the practices of literary interpretation used in reading poetry or fiction; on the other hand, they study practices that urban youth use in other contexts—for example, in music or in conversation. Lee and her colleagues then build instructional connections between the practices in which students are already engaged and structurally similar practices that are necessary to literary interpretation.

Investigations of mathematical activity in out-of-school contexts similar to those that Lee and her colleagues studied might enable the construction of similar instructional mappings between out-of-school and in-school practices. Students, especially those who traditionally have not acquired mathematical proficiency, could be helped to connect their out-of-school practices of calculating, reasoning, and representing with the mathematical problem-solving practices expected of them in school. For example, the notational systems that some young people invent to keep track of the scores in a complex game can reflect substantial sensitivity and skill in what it takes to construct and use representations of changing quantities. Such representational practices that are developed outside of school could be built upon as teachers help students acquire skill and fluency with mathematical notation.

A second reason for the focus on practices involved in doing and learning mathematics centers on the current demands of everyday life. As we enter the 21st century, many individuals have expressed a renewed concern for the kind of mathematical proficiency needed in a world flooded with quantitative information that requires decisionmaking using such information and that demands

---

[7]Lee & Majors, 2000.

extensive use of spatial reasoning.[8] Mathematics is increasingly needed for analysis and interpretation of information in domains as varied as politics, business, economics, social policy, and science policy.

Knowing and using mathematics is critical to a functional citizenry and the empowerment of all members of society. We believe that such knowledge and use requires what we have termed "mathematical practices." Because the broad and effective development of mathematical proficiency is the fundamental goal of school mathematics education, we argue that a focus on understanding the mathematical practices that are required beyond one's school years should be a critical component of the proposed research and development agenda.

This requirement for proficiency gives rise to a third reason for the proposed focus on mathematical practices. These practices provide learning resources needed by teachers and students who are engaged in more ambitious curricula and who are working toward more-complex educational goals. Without these resources, ambitious agendas for improvement in mathematics education are unlikely to succeed. When higher standards for student performance are set, educators know little about what students and teachers would have to do, and learn to do, to meet those standards. What it would take for all students and teachers to achieve such ambitious goals has not been adequately examined. Consequently, despite greater expectations and important new goals, student performance may not improve. For example, when a teacher who never before has asked her students to explain their thinking suddenly asks those students to justify their solutions, she is likely to be greeted with silence. When she asks a student to explain a method he has used, he will probably think that he made an error. And when teachers assign more-challenging work, students who are unsure of what to do may ask for so much help that the tasks' cognitive demands on the student are reduced.[9] Teachers who do not know how to produce mathematical explanations or choose useful representations for solving a problem may lack the necessary resources for helping students. Discouraged, teachers may conclude that their students cannot do more-complex work and may return to simpler tasks.

In sum, our emphasis on investigating mathematical practices offers a means for uncovering what has to be understood in order for students to learn and do mathematics proficiently. Uncovering these practices can make it possible to design systematic opportunities for students (and teachers) to develop the

---

[8]See, for example, Banchoff, 1988; Devlin, 1999; National Research Council, 1989; Paulos, 1988, 1991, 1996; Rothstein, 1995; and Steen, 2001.

[9]Stein, Grover, & Henningsen, 1996.

learning resources needed to build a system in which all students can become mathematically proficient.

WHAT DO WE NEED TO KNOW ABOUT LEARNING AND TEACHING MATHEMATICAL PRACTICES?

The RAND Mathematics Study Panel's proposal for a focus on mathematical practices reflects the conviction that this focus would yield crucial insights that are needed to close the broad gap between those few who become mathematically proficient and the many who do not. Building knowledge about mathematical practices would help to make visible and connect the crucial elements of mathematical proficiency, the acquisition of which has been unsystematic and uneven.

The proposed focus on mathematical practices can build on significant prior research related to specific mathematical practices. While the general notion of "mathematical practices" may be an unfamiliar one to some people, we believe progress can be made by grouping together aspects of mathematical practices that have usually been treated separately and investigating aspects of their use, learning, and instruction that have remained unevenly explored. The proposed research and development on mathematical practices would focus on *activity*— the work of *learning* and *doing* mathematics. It would also take a more social view of these practices by examining them as activities of doing mathematics in interaction with other activities in specific settings, as well as examining them as cognitive processes in which individuals engage when they do mathematics. This perspective is important because practices are often acquired and enacted through interaction with others in a mathematical activity.

Where should investments be made if a focus on mathematical practices is to have the payoff that we envision? First, rather than plunging into an unmapped territory of unnamed and undefined mathematical practices, we argue that the most progress will be made in the short term if the work concentrates on three core practices that have already been the subject of substantial research: representation, justification, and generalization. These three practices are arguably central to the learning and use of mathematics in a wide range of classroom and everyday settings, and new work done in these areas can build on established research.

The domain of *representation* includes the choices one makes in expressing and depicting mathematical ideas and the ways in which one puts those choices to use. The decimal representation of numbers (using place values), for example, is one of the most important historical examples of representation. For example, consider the difference between the Roman numeral representation of the year 1776 (MDCCLXXVI) and its base-ten representation. Representation also includes modeling, in which a physical situation is described in mathematical terms, such as Newton's formulation of gravitational attraction. Representing ideas in a variety of ways is fundamental to mathematical work. No one ideal representation exists because the quality of a representation depends on the purpose of the representation.

For example, a rational number can be represented as many different fractions and also as a repeating or terminating decimal. Three-fourths can be represented as 3/4, but also as 6/8, 9/12, or 273/364. It is easier to compare 4/5 with 13/16 if the numbers are represented in decimal form (0.8 and 0.8125, respectively). What is less apparent from the decimal form is the commensurability of the two numbers—i.e., the difference between 3/4 and 2/3 is more readily apparent if the fractions were represented with 12 as the denominator. Likewise, whole numbers—take 60, for instance—can be represented in base-ten place value notation (i.e., 60). But the prime factorization of 60 (i.e., $2^2 \times 3 \times 5$) is more informative for some purposes—such as finding the greatest common divisors—because it makes the multiplicative structure of the number visible in a way that the place-value representation does not. Choosing which representations to use depends on the work one wants to do with the mathematical objects in question. Fourth-graders learn that representing 5,002 as 499 tens and 12 ones makes it easier to compute 5,002 minus 169. Rewriting numbers is a critical part of the practice of representation.

Another critical practice—the fluent use of symbolic notation—is included in the domain of representational practice. Mathematics employs a unique and highly developed symbolic language upon which many forms of mathematical work and thinking depend. Symbolic notation allows for precision in expression. It is also efficient—it compresses complex ideas into a form that makes them easier to comprehend and manipulate. Mathematics learning and use is critically dependent on one's being able to fluently and flexibly encode ideas and relationships. Equally important is the ability to accurately decode what others have written.

A second core mathematical practice for which we recommend research and development is the work of justifying claims, solutions, and methods. *Justification* centers on how mathematical knowledge is certified and established as "knowledge." Understanding a mathematical idea means both knowing it and also knowing why it is true. For example, knowing that rolling a 7 with two dice is more likely than rolling a 12 is different from being able to explain why this is so. Although "understanding" is part of contemporary education reform rhetoric, the reasoning of justification, upon which understanding critically depends, is largely missing in much mathematics teaching and learning. Many students, even those at university level, lack not only the capacity to construct proofs—the mathematician's form of justification—but even lack an appreciation of what a mathematical proof is. Mathematical justification involves reasoning that is more general than what we typically call "proof." In everyday situations, being able to support the validity of a mathematical conclusion also matters.

Justification is a practice supported by both intellectual tools and mental "habits." These tools and habits are grounded in valuing a cluster of questions about knowing something and what it takes to be certain: Why does this work? Is this true? How do I know? Can I convince other people that it is true? Such questions apply not only to sophisticated mathematical claims but also to the results of the most-elementary observations and procedures.

The third core area of practice the panel proposes for research and development is generalization. Generalization involves searching for patterns, structures, and relationships in data or mathematical symbols. These patterns, structures, and relationships transcend the particulars of the data or symbols and point to more-general conclusions that can be made about all data or symbols in a particular class. Hypothesizing and testing generalizations about observations or data is a critical part of problem solving.

In one of the simpler common exercises designed to develop young students' capabilities to generalize, students are presented with a series of numbers and are asked to predict what the next number in the series will be. To do this, they must find the pattern in the number series that permits them to calculate the next number in the series.

Representational practices play an important role in generalizing. For example, being able to represent an odd number as $2k+1$ shows that the general structure of an odd number is such that when dividing the number into two equal parts, there is always one left over. This structure is true for all odd numbers. Representing the structure using symbolic notation permits a direct view of the general form. This example suggests that a variety of discrete practices are often combined in mathematical reasoning or practice.

As with representation, the capabilities for generalization are based on both tools and habits that guide individuals or groups in identifying patterns in the world around them. Mathematics education provides a domain in which tools and habits can be developed concerning generalization that can be applied to commonplace tasks in everyday life.

Using these three core practices as a basic starting point, we recommend support for three lines of concentrated work:

- Developing a fuller understanding of specific mathematical practices, including how they interact and how they matter in different mathematical domains

- Examining the use of these mathematical practices in different settings: practices that are used in various aspects of schooling, students' out-of-school practices, and practices employed by adults in their everyday and work lives

- Investigating ways in which these specific mathematical practices can be developed in classrooms and the role these practices play as a component of a teachers' mathematical resources.

Past work on problem solving, reasoning, and other processes has tended to view the three practices separately and, consequently, knowledge of how these processes interconnect with one another is not well developed. How, for example, do students' approaches to representation shape their efforts to prove claims? Additionally, little research has compared specific processes across mathematical domains. For example, how do students' efforts to use representations in algebra differ from their use of pictorial representations in arithmetic? How do students approach proof in arithmetic versus proof in geometry? How does learning to employ the representational tools of algebra — i.e., symbols— help students to engage in justification of claims in probability? We should seek to uncover how these particular practices differ, and how they are similar, across different mathematical domains.

Because we want to develop insights that can help students make connections between the mathematics they use outside of school and what it means to do mathematics skillfully, research is needed to uncover the mathematical practices that students use in settings outside of school. In particular, activities that involve patterning and repetition, notation and other systems of recording, calculation, construction, and arrangement could be identified. How explanations are sought and developed and how conclusions are justified also would be of interest. Children's activities and performance in various settings could be observed, described with precision, and analyzed to uncover the mathematics-related practices that are important in these settings.

Similar investigations are needed of adults' everyday practices and their practices in the work world. Better understanding of the ways in which adults use (or could use) mathematics in a variety of settings—in their work and in the course of their everyday adult life—would extend the knowledge about practices that are important to mathematical proficiency. Situations that call for mathematical reasoning arise in domains as varied as personal health (e.g., weighing the costs and benefits of new drug treatments), citizenship (e.g., understanding the effect of changes in voting procedures on election outcomes), personal finance, professional practices, and work tasks. The (often-invisible) uses of mathematics and mathematical practices in everyday situations are fascinating. Some common examples involve money (e.g., calculating tips), cooking (e.g., measuring ingredients), home decorating (e.g., figuring out the number of tiles needed for a bathroom floor), playing games of chance (e.g., estimating probabilities), and reading newspapers and magazines (e.g., interpreting data in tables and graphs).

Many adult jobs require the use of mathematics. Some are in mathematically intensive professions such as engineering, nursing, banking, and teaching, but some are in a host of other occupations in which workers must employ a range of mathematical skills and practices (e.g., waiting tables, carpentry, tailoring, or even operating a sandwich cart).[10] This focus in the proposed research and development program should include investigations of the practices used in various work environments to build a broad perspective on mathematical practices that are important to learning and using mathematics. One role of such investigations is that they can make important contributions to setting future standards for mathematics proficiency.

While most existing research has focused on how students engage in these practices, less is known about how their use of particular practices develops over time. Even less attention has been paid to the teaching involved in developing these practices. For example, most research on the subject of proof examines how students approach the task of proving a claim, what they accept as a proof, and what convinces them that a statement is true. Much less has been developed to inform instructional practice related to proof. What does it take to help students to learn to engage in practices of justification? What sorts of tasks contribute to learning, and are there characteristics of instruction that help to build students' effectiveness with particular practices? What are the features of classrooms and classroom activities that make it possible for students to develop and engage in mathematical practices? What features, specifically, shape the learning of different students? How can opportunities for the development and use of mathematical practices be designed to engage students who have traditionally avoided or not performed well in mathematics in school?

Many educators assume that simply offering students instructional tasks that implicitly call for such practices will lead students to engage in those practices. We hypothesize that such practices must be deliberately cultivated and developed, and therefore research and development should be devoted to addressing this challenge.

---

[10]See, for example, Hall & Stevens, 1995; Hoyles, Noss, & Pozzi, 2001; and Noss & Hoyles, 1996.

Finally, the way in which mathematical practices affect the knowledge it takes to teach remains largely unexamined. How do teachers' own capacities for representation or justification shape their instructional effectiveness? Under what circumstances does the need to use these practices appear in the course of teaching? For example, when teachers use a board to set up problems, display solutions, or record students' work, how well are they able to represent mathematical ideas, how skillful are they with notation, and how well do they use representations to support students' discussions and classroom work? The place of mathematical practices in the resources that teachers deploy in teaching has been, for the most part, unexplored and should prove to be a fruitful area for investigation.

Chapter Four

TEACHING AND LEARNING ALGEBRA IN KINDERGARTEN THROUGH 12TH GRADE

The way in which a mathematics curriculum is organized shapes students' opportunity to learn. A research agenda aimed at understanding and supporting the development of mathematical proficiency should examine the ways in which mathematics instruction is organized. It should do so by looking closely at the organization and presentation of particular mathematical topics and skills in the school curriculum.

Mathematics teaching and learning are probably best studied within specific mathematical domains and contexts, but there may be aspects of mathematics teaching and learning that are more general and can be studied across multiple domains and contexts. Where systematic inquiry focused on learning specific areas of mathematics has been conducted previously—for example, research on children's early learning of numbers, addition, and subtraction—the payoff for teaching and learning has been substantial.[1] This experience suggests that it would be fruitful to focus coordinated research on how students learn within other topical domains of school mathematics. This research should include studies of how understanding, skill, and the ability to use knowledge in those domains develop over time. It should also include studies of how such learning is shaped by variations in the instruction students are offered, by the ways that instruction is organized within schools, and by the broader policy and environmental contexts that affect the ways schools work.

For a number of reasons, which we discuss next, the RAND Mathematics Study Panel recommends that the initial topical choice for focused and coordinated research and development should be algebra. We define algebra broadly to include the way in which it develops throughout the kindergarten through 12th grade (K–12) curriculum and its relationship to other mathematical topics upon which algebra builds and to which it is connected.

---

[1] Kilpatrick, Swafford, & Findell, 2001.

ALGEBRA AS A MATHEMATICAL DOMAIN AND SCHOOL SUBJECT

We use the term "algebra" to broadly cover the mathematical ideas and tools that constitute this major branch of the discipline, including classical topics and modern extensions of the subject. Algebra is foundational in all areas of mathematics because it provides the tools (i.e., the language and structure) for representing and analyzing quantitative relationships, for modeling situations, for solving problems, and for stating and proving generalizations. An important aspect of algebra in contemporary mathematics is its capacity to provide general and unifying mathematical concepts. This capacity is a powerful resource for building coherence and connectivity in the school mathematics curriculum, across grade levels, and across mathematical settings.

Historically, algebra began with the introduction of letter symbols in arithmetic expressions to represent names of undetermined quantities. These symbols might be "unknowns" in an equation to be solved or the variables in a functional relationship. As the ideas and uses of algebra have expanded, it has come to include structural descriptions of number systems and their generalizations, and also the basic notions of functions and their use for modeling empirical phenomena—for example, as a way of encoding emergent patterns observed in data. Algebra systematizes the construction and analysis of the formulas, equations, and functions that make up much of mathematics and its applications. Algebra, both as a mathematical domain and as a school subject, has come to embrace all of these themes.

Researchers have made many recommendations about the appropriate curricular focus for school algebra, as well as what constitutes proficiency in K–12 algebra.[2] Common to most of these recommendations are the following expectations related to algebraic proficiency:

- The ability to work flexibly and meaningfully with formulas or algebraic relations—to use them to represent situations, to manipulate them, and to solve the equations they represent

- A structural understanding of the basic operations of arithmetic and of the notational representations of numbers and mathematical operations (for example, place value, fraction notation, exponentiation)

- A robust understanding of the notion of function, including representing functions (for example, tabular, analytic, and graphical forms); having a

---

[2]See, for example, National Council of Teachers of Mathematics, 2000; Achieve, 2002; Learning First Alliance, 1998; and various state mathematics frameworks (for example, a mathematics framework for California at www.cde.ca.gov/board/pdf/math.pdf, a mathematics framework for Georgia at www.doe.k12.ga.us/sla/ret/math-grades-1-8-edited.pdf, and a mathematics framework for Illinois at www.isbe.net/ils/math/math.html).

good repertoire of the basic functions (linear and quadratic polynomials, and exponential, rational, and trigonometric functions); and using functions to study the change of one quantity in relation to another

- Knowing how to identify and name significant variables to model quantitative contexts, recognizing patterns, and using symbols, formulas, and functions to represent those contexts.

These recommendations also call for the concepts of algebra to be coherently connected across the primary and secondary school years and for instruction that makes these connections. Consistent with both the direction of state and national frameworks and standards, and the visible trends in instructional materials used across the United States, our proposed research would examine the teaching and learning of algebra and related foundational ideas and skills beginning with the primary and extending through the secondary levels.

For example, when five-year-olds investigate the relationships among colored wooden rods of different lengths, they are gaining experience with the fundamental notions of proportionality and measure, an instance of using models to understand quantitative relationships. When, as six-year-olds, they represent these relationships symbolically, they are developing the mathematical sensibilities and skills that can prepare them for learning algebraic notation later on. And when seven-year-olds "skip count"—for example, count by twos starting with the number three (3, 5, 7, and so forth)—they may be gaining experience with basic ideas of linear relationships, which are foundational for understanding patterns, relations, and functions.

At the middle school level, connections of proportional reasoning with geometry and measurement appear in the following sort of analysis: If one doubles the length, width, and depth of a swimming pool, then it takes about twice the number of tiles to border the top edge of the pool, four times the amount of paint to cover the sides and bottom, and eight times the amount of water to fill the pool.

At the high school level, the following example illustrates several of the previous motifs simultaneously. Consider the temperature, T, of a container of ice cream removed from a freezer and left in a warm room. The change in T over time t (measured from the time of removal) can be modeled as a function,

$$T(t) = a - b2^{-t} + b$$

where a and b are constants and b is positive. By transforming this formula algebraically to the form

$$T(t) = a + b(1 - 2^{-t})$$

and using knowledge of the exponential function, we can see that T(t) increases from a at time t = 0 toward $a + b$ as time advances. This is because as t gets larger, 2^{-t} decreases toward zero. Many mathematicians and educators would agree that students should reach a level of proficiency that enables them to see what a and $a + b$ each represents—that is, the freezer temperature and the room temperature, respectively. This level of proficiency involves understanding what it means for this formula to model the phenomenon in question and transforming the formula algebraically to make certain features of the phenomena being modeled more visible. It also involves interpreting the terms in the formula and understanding what the formula says about the phenomena that it models.

In this case, the formula for T was given, and it was analyzed algebraically. But how does one find such formulas in the first place? This is the (usually more difficult) empirical phase of modeling a phenomenon, in which one gathers some data—say, a set of measurements of T at certain moments in time, perhaps delivered from some electronic data source—and then selects a function from his or her repertoire that best models the data. This process can be quite complex but is often feasible with the use of technology for most of the models typically included in school curricula. The education community is in the midst of a period of important changes in school algebra, with shifting and contending views about who should take it, when they should learn it, what it should cover, and how it should be taught. As recently as ten years ago, the situation was more stable: Generally, algebra was the province of college-bound students, primarily those headed for careers in the sciences. Algebra was taken as a distinct course first encountered in high school; it focused on structures and procedures and often the teaching emphasized procedural fluency and competency in manipulation of symbols.

Today's school algebra is construed by a variety of people, including mathematicians, businesspeople, mathematics educators, and policymakers, to be a broader field encompassing a wider range of subjects. Many people think it should be required of all students, not just a select few, and that it should be addressed across the grades, not only in high school. Teachers and developers of instructional materials are now committed to helping students learn algebra in such a way that it is meaningful and applicable in a wide range of contexts. In addition, the technological tools (e.g., graphing calculators and computer-based algebra tutors) available to help students understand and use algebra have changed radically. Today's school algebra is dynamic in every way.

BENEFITS OF A FOCUS ON ALGEBRA

We selected algebra as an initial area of focus for the proposed research and development program for three main reasons.

First, as we discussed earlier, algebra is fundamental for exploring most areas of mathematics, science, and engineering. Algebraic notation, thinking, and concepts are also important in a number of workplace contexts and in the interpretation of information that individuals receive in their daily lives.

A second reason for selecting algebra as an initial area of focus is its unique and formidable gatekeeper role in K–12 schooling. Without proficiency in algebra, students cannot access a full range of educational and career options, and they have limited chances of success. Failure to learn algebra is widespread, and the consequences of this failure are that far too many students are disenfranchised. This curtailment of opportunity falls most directly on groups that are already disadvantaged and exacerbates existing inequities in our society. Moses and Cobb argue forcefully that algebra should be regarded as "the new civil right" accessible to all U.S. citizens:[3]

> . . . once solely in place as the gatekeeper for higher math and the priesthood who gained access to it, [algebra] now is the gatekeeper for citizenship, and people who don't have it are like the people who couldn't read and write in the industrial age . . . . [Lack of access to algebra] has become not a barrier to college entrance, but a barrier to citizenship. That's the importance of algebra that has emerged with the new higher technology.

Finally, many U.S. high schools now require students to demonstrate substantial proficiency in algebra before they can graduate. These requirements are a result of the higher standards for mathematics that are being adopted by most states as a result of the general public pressure for higher standards and associated accountability systems. The recent "No Child Left Behind" legislation has reinforced these moves. The significant increase in performance expectations in algebra proficiency associated with these standards imposes challenges for students and teachers alike. In the near term, a lack of strong and usable research in support of instructional improvement in algebra is likely to lead to interventions and policy decisions that are fragmented and unsystematic. These interventions will be vulnerable to the polemics of a divisive political environment. In the longer term, research and development coupled with trial and evaluation are needed to create new materials, instructional skills, and programs that will enable the attainment of higher standards for mathematical proficiency.

---

[3]Moses & Cobb, 2001.

Other domains of mathematics, such as probability, statistics, or geometry, might vie for focused attention, along with algebra, in our proposed research and development program. Each of these domains is important, and strong arguments could be made for why each would be a good focus for coordinated work. We expect that, over time, systematic work would be supported in these areas. Still, algebra occupies a special place among the various domains because it is more than a topical domain. It provides linguistic and representational tools for work throughout mathematics. It is a strategic choice for addressing equity issues in mathematics education, and its centrality and political prominence make it a logical choice for a first focus within a new, coordinated program of research and development.

WHAT DO WE NEED TO KNOW ABOUT TEACHING AND LEARNING ALGEBRA?

Algebra is an area in which significant educational research has already been conducted. Since the 1970s, researchers in the United States, and around the world, have systematically studied questions about student learning in algebra and have accumulated very useful knowledge about the difficulties and misunderstandings that students have in this domain. Researchers have looked at student understanding of literal terms and expressions, simplifying expressions, equations, word problems, and functions and graphs.[4] This previous work that highlights student thinking patterns and the difficulties that students typically have with algebra is invaluable as a foundation for what is needed now.

Despite the extensive research in this area, we lack research on what is happening today in algebra classrooms; how innovations in algebra teaching and learning can be designed, implemented, and assessed; and how policy decisions can shape student learning and improve equity. Because most studies have focused on algebra at the high school level, we know little about younger students' learning of algebraic ideas and skills. Little is known about what happens when algebra is viewed as a K–12 subject, is integrated with other subjects, or emphasizes a wider range of concepts and processes. Research could inform the perennial debates about what to include, emphasize, reduce, or omit. We see the proposed algebra research agenda as having three major components:

- Analyses and comparison of curriculum, instruction, and assessment

- Studies of the relationships among teaching, instructional materials, and learning

- Studies of the impact of policy contexts on equity and student learning.

---

[4]Kieran, 1992.

Analyses and Comparison of Curriculum, Instruction, and Assessment

There is much debate and disagreement today over what topics, concepts, skills, and procedures should be included in school algebra. However, the debate is often based on conjecture and unsupported assumptions about what is going on in the nation's schools in the area of algebra. Our proposed research agenda includes a call for a description and analysis of the goals, areas of emphasis, topics, and sequencing of algebra as they are represented in the various curricula, instructional approaches, frameworks, and assessments currently in use. Algebra curricula today risk being categorized in oversimplified ways according to the "perspectives" on algebra they embody (e.g., "functions-based," "generalized arithmetic," or "real-world" perspectives).

Researchers could provide critically important analytic frameworks and tools for the systematic description and comparison of the curricular treatments of algebra and go on to conduct this description and comparison on a national scale. Perhaps the "pure" embodiments of these various perspectives will turn out to be relatively rare. It may be that many instructional materials integrate various perspectives into complex constructions that involve intricate decisions about sequencing and emphasis on and motivation of ideas. In short, discussions about the nature of school algebra could be much more productive if more-refined tools and analytic frameworks were available. Some tools, such as surveys and other instruments, and methodologies for such large-scale descriptive work already exist.[5] Likewise, a number of scholars and professional groups have offered ways of categorizing and describing perspectives on school algebra.[6] We need systematic, reliable information on how algebra is actually represented in contemporary elementary and secondary curriculum materials, as designed and as enacted.

Despite the flurry of intense debates over algebra, we know far too little about the relevant aspects of what is happening in the schools. We know little about which instructional materials and tools are used in the nation's classrooms for the teaching of algebra, how teachers use these materials in their practice, or how student learning of algebra is assessed. How much has the algebra curriculum actually changed at the high school level? How much have the ideas and tools of algebra, from any perspective, permeated the elementary school curriculum? How do elementary and secondary teachers understand and use algebra, and what perspectives of this domain typify their knowledge? Large-

---

[5]For example, The Third International Mathematics and Science Study (TIMSS) Curriculum Framework (see Mullis et al., 2001); the "Study of Instructional Improvement" (2000) and other alignment frameworks such as the framework described by Porter & Smithson, 2001.

[6]See, for example, Chazan, 2000; Bednarz, Kieran, & Lee, 1996; Kaput, 1998b; Lacampagne, Blair, & Kaput, 1995.

scale descriptive studies might examine such areas as teachers' use of textbooks, the ways in which technologies are used in algebra classrooms, what tools and approaches teachers draw on in algebra instruction, and how the ideas of algebra are integrated with other areas of mathematics.

Before recommendations for change and improvement in the teaching of algebra can be fully realized, and in order to invest most strategically in widespread intervention, educators, policymakers, funders, and researchers need to understand the current state of affairs in the nation's classrooms. In addition, we also lack knowledge of what students learn with different versions of algebra—what skills they develop, what understanding of algebra they have, and what they are able to do with algebraic ideas and tools. Yet, most assessments are built on strong assumptions about when students should study algebra and what they should learn. Analytic work can make these assumptions more explicit and clarify the consequences of misalignment between what students are being taught and what high-stakes assessments are demanding.

Studies of Relationships Among Teaching, Instructional Materials, and Learning

The desired outcome of this proposed agenda of research and development is for the nation's students to understand algebra and be able to use it. Achieving this outcome will mean (1) selecting key ideas of algebra and algebraic ways of thinking to be developed over the K–12 spectrum; (2) designing, testing, and adapting instructional treatments and curricular arrangements to help students learn those ideas and ways of thinking; and (3) assessing the outcomes. Each of these choices would need to be described, articulated, measured, and related to student learning, and high-quality evidence would need to be collected to study the impact of various designs. The strategy we envision involves designing particular instructional approaches and comparing them with existing regimes, as well as with one another. Such systematic work would permit the development of knowledge and tools for the teaching and learning of algebra at various levels and over time. Several considerations and areas of focus, which we discuss next, should shape the organization of work in this part of the research agenda.

Given the range of perspectives about what should constitute school algebra, there is space in this agenda for research that develops curricular and instructional approaches that play out and test the implications of particular perspectives. For example, Carpenter and his colleagues have adopted the view that the teaching of arithmetic can serve as a foundation for the learning of algebra.[7] Their research explores how developing elementary students' capacity to exam-

---

[7]Carpenter & Levi, 1999.

ine, test, and verify or discard conjectures can support important learning about mathematical relations, language, and representation. Building on existing work,[8] other perspectives on algebra need to be developed and studied, such as instruction that follows the historical evolution of algebra, or instruction that takes geometry, rather than arithmetic, as a starting point for instruction in algebra.[9] To illustrate how basic ideas of algebraic structure have been introduced to middle school students from a geometric perspective, consider the following example:[10]

> You are going to build a square garden and surround its border with square tiles. Each tile is 1 foot by 1 foot. For example, if the dimensions of the garden are 10 feet by 10 feet, then you will need 44 tiles for the border.

> How many tiles would you need for a garden that is n feet by n feet?

Teachers have found that students will generate many expressions in response to this question,[11] often with strong and clear connections to the actual physical representations of the situation. For example, one correct answer is 4n + 4, which students will explain by noting that there are four sides, each of which is n feet in length—the "4n" counts the tiles needed along each of the four sides, and the "+ 4" picks up the corners. This is illustrated by the diagram at the left below (when n = 3). Two other representations that would be correct (when n = 3) are also shown below.

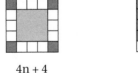

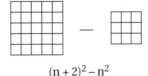

4n + 4   4(n + 1) $(n + 2)^2 - n^2$

---

[8]See, for example, Chazan, 2000; Gallardo, 2001; and Heid, 1996.

[9]Wheeler, 1996, p. 318.

[10]Adapted from Lappan et al., 1998, p. 20.

[11]See Phillips & Lappan, 1998, and Ferrini-Mundy, Lappan, & Phillips, 1996.

Because these different algebraic expressions represent the same physical quantity (the number of tiles needed), students can use the geometry to establish their equivalence. Here, the geometric perspective introduces students to early ideas of algebraic structure.

Language plays a crucial role in algebra, and so a program of research in this area should include work on language. Words used in algebra—*distribute, factor, model,* and even *plus* and *minus*—are familiar to students from other contexts. In commenting on algebra research, Wheeler[12] asks, "What happens to one's interpretation of the plus sign . . . when it is placed between two symbols which *cannot* be combined and replaced by another symbol?" That is, what do students make of the algebraic *expression a + b* after years of being able to compress expressions such as 3 + 5 into the single number 8?[13] Algebra may be a key site for the development of students' mathematical language, where the translation of everyday experiences into abstract representations is essential. Problems with language may affect English-language learners in different ways than it affects students for whom English is a second language.[14]

It will also be important for researchers to solicit projects designed to examine the connections among significant ideas within different treatments of algebra. For instance, there is a base of research about students' understanding of function[15] that reveals difficulties that students have in distinguishing functions from other relations and in interpreting graphical representations of functions. Yet, we know little about the relationship between a student's understanding of how functions relate and ideas such as correlation and curve fitting in data analysis. How can teachers and instructional materials effectively make links between related mathematical ideas so that students' knowledge builds systematically over time? Algebra is replete with instances where connections are likely to help build students' understanding. Consider the fact that many students may learn to manipulate x's and y's and never realize that x^2 has a geometric representation—a square with a side length of x. They do not recognize that they can visualize the difference between $x^2 + y^2$ and $(x + y)^2$ quite simply with a diagram, such as the following:

---

[12]Wheeler, 1996, p. 324.

[13]See Collis, 1975.

[14]See Moschkovich, 1999; Khisty, 1997; Secada, 1990; Gutiérrez, 2002a.

[15]See Harel & Dubinsky, 1992, and Leinhardt, Zaslavsky, & Stein, 1990.

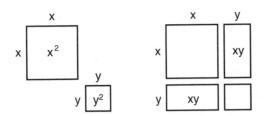

As the example illustrations in this chapter suggest, connections between different areas of mathematics—algebra and arithmetic, algebra and geometry, or algebra and statistics—can be fruitfully examined using algebra as a domain for research.

Research and development should focus on how algebra can be taught and learned effectively across the elementary and secondary years. This will involve substantial longitudinal and cross-sectional comparative work. Certain ideas can be introduced early and come to play key roles in more-advanced algebra learning.

We know, for instance, both from research and from the experience of teachers, that the notion of "equal" is complex and difficult for students to comprehend, and it is also a central mathematical idea within algebra. The equals sign (=) is used to indicate the equality of the values of two expressions. When a variable x is involved, the equals sign may denote the equivalence of two functions (equal values for all values of x), or it may indicate an equation to be solved—that is, finding all values of x for which the functions take the same value. Many studies of students' understanding and use of equality and equation solving[16] have shown that students come to high school algebra with confused notions of equality. For instance, some students think of an equals sign not as a statement of equivalence but as a signal to perform an operation, presumably based on experience in the elementary school years with problems such as 8 + 4 = ____. In fact, some secondary students will, at the beginning of their algebra studies, fill in the blank in "8 + 4 = ____ + 3" with 12. Researchers have suggested that this tendency comes as a result of children's experience in executing arithmetic operations and writing down an answer immediately to the right of an equals sign.

The powerful abstract concepts and notation of algebra allow the expression of ideas and generalized relationships. Equally central to the value of algebra is the set of rules for manipulating these ideas and relationships. These concepts, notation, and rules for manipulation are invaluable for solving a wide range of problems. Learning to make sense of and operate meaningfully and effectively

---

[16]See, for example, Kieran, 1981, and Wagner, 1981.

with algebraic procedures presents formidable challenges to learning and teaching.

It is especially challenging for teachers to motivate student interest and to foster persistence in this work on symbolic fluency that is so central to algebraic proficiency. Researchers, developers, and practitioners alike ask how such capacity is effectively fostered over time. For example, what kinds of meaning can be attached to symbols and manipulations to support the learning of their use and significance? Although some algebraic relations can be modeled experientially, others are essentially abstract or formal in character. In cases in which the relations are more abstract, meaning can often be located in the very patterns and structure of the formulas and operations themselves. And what levels of skill or fluency are appropriate for various grades or courses? For instance, the proficiency in manipulation of algebraic symbols that should be expected of a beginning calculus student is probably more elaborate and developed than what would be expected of an eighth-grade student. Compelling arguments can be made that procedural fluency is enhanced by intense use. But such intense use could also be designed as part of conceptual explorations of mathematical problems or as part of carrying out mathematical projects, and indeed has been addressed this way in many recent curricular treatments of algebra.

Another current issue that is closely related to the development of symbolic fluency is how different instructional uses of technology interact with the development of algebra skills and algebraic concepts. The increased availability of technology raises new questions about what is meant by "symbolic fluency." Research suggests that graphing calculators and computer algebra systems are promising tools for supporting certain kinds of understanding in algebra, including understanding of algebraic representations.[17] At the same time, important questions remain about the role of paper-and-pencil computation in developing understanding as well as skill. These are questions that appear at every level of school mathematics. Empirical investigation and evidence are essential for practitioners who need stronger evidence for making wise instructional decisions.

Research about algebra has focused more closely on student learning issues than on algebra teaching issues. As Kieran (1992) notes, "The research community knows very little about how algebra teachers teach algebra and what their conceptions are of their own students' learning."[18] For the ambitious changes in algebra instruction and curriculum that are underway nationally to be effective, teachers, teacher educators, and developers of instructional materials need

---

[17]See Heid, 1997, and Kilpatrick, Swafford & Findell, 2001.

[18]Kieran, 1992, p. 395.

research-based information about different models for algebra teaching at different levels and the impact of those models on student learning of different aspects of algebra. Moreover, research could uncover ways in which teachers work, how they use particular opportunities to learn, and how they use instructional materials, and the like, as they plan and teach lessons. For example, although elementary teachers' use of texts has been investigated in various studies, less is known about how algebra teachers use textbooks, tools, technology, and other instructional materials. Yet, such knowledge would be critical to any large-scale improvement of algebra learning for U.S. students in that it would guide the design and implementation of instructional programs.

In summary, the changing algebra education landscape demands that we direct collective research energies toward solving some of the most pressing problems that are emerging as a result of these change. Research into algebra teaching, learning, and instructional materials should be at the forefront of efforts to improve outcomes for all students in learning algebra in the nation's K–12 classrooms.

IMPACT OF POLICY CONTEXTS ON STUDENT LEARNING

A focus on algebra also brings us squarely to issues related to the organization of the curriculum in U.S. schools, to the requirements for course taking and high school graduation, and to the uses of assessments for purposes of accountability that have far-reaching consequences. All of these policy-context issues relate in crucial ways to matters of equity, students' opportunities to learn, and the prospects for all students in U.S. schools to have a wide range of choices in their professional and personal lives. Thus, research is crucial for better understanding the implications and results of various policy choices and the range of curricular and structural choices (when algebra is taken and by whom, for example) made by schools and districts at a time when the pressures and demands on teachers, administrators, and state and local policymakers are considerable and conflicting.

In the high school and middle school curriculum of U.S. schools, algebra is typically treated as a separate course, and currently most of the material in that course is new to students. In contrast, mathematics in the elementary schools typically combines student experiences with several different mathematical domains. These traditions have recently been challenged by analyses showing that the secondary curricula in most other countries do not isolate algebra within a course apart from other topic areas.[19] The elementary and middle school curricula in most other countries treat algebra more extensively than do

---

[19]Schmidt et al., 1997.

the curricula in the United States. Many of the instructional materials developed in the United States in the past decade include greater integration of content areas and topics at the secondary school level and greater attention being paid to algebra at the elementary and middle school levels.

Research can address how these various curricular arrangements influence students' learning and their decisions to participate in subsequent courses. If algebra begins to permeate the elementary curriculum in the coming decade, how will its curricular trajectory in the middle and secondary schools change? Such changes will have important implications for the assessment of algebraic proficiency. Algebra's curricular scope—whether located in the traditional high school course sequence or expanded across the grades—presents important questions about the mathematical education opportunities available to diverse populations of students whose prior success with school mathematics has varied dramatically.

Because algebra has been identified as a critical gatekeeper experience, schools and districts struggle with questions about whether algebra should be required of all students and whether it should be offered in the eighth grade. There is some research to indicate that early access to algebra may improve both achievement and disposition toward taking advanced mathematics.[20] Yet, there is no robust body of work to support decisionmakers in school districts on this matter, and the issues are quite complex. For instance, school districts that have adopted a policy that all ninth-graders take algebra typically have eliminated general mathematics, consumer mathematics, and pre-algebra courses. This seems like a positive step toward raising standards for all students, and a direction that should lead to greater equity for students who have traditionally (and disproportionately) occupied the lower-level courses. Some research suggests this has indeed been the case.[21]

However, a program of research aimed at better understanding the issues surrounding algebra education should address the more subtle aspects of such policy shifts and the range of interpretations and implementations due to this shift in policy. For instance, some schools have responded with first-year algebra courses that span two years and that fulfill the high school mathematics requirement, getting students no further than if they had taken algebra in grade ten. And teachers faced with the challenge of heterogeneous classes of algebra students coming from a wide range of pre-algebra instruction and experiences, and possibly unconvinced of the wisdom that all students should study algebra, may need considerable support and professional development to deliver a

---

[20]See Smith, 1996.

[21]See, for instance, Gamoran et al., 1997, and Lee & Smith, forthcoming.

course that meets the high standards for the subject. Thus, new research work is needed to help illuminate the nature and range of trends in the implementation of certain policies, as well as the consequences for student learning and continuing successful participation in mathematics. Algebra has assumed a critical political and social position in the curriculum; research can help explain the implications of this position.

Research has demonstrated that taking algebra in the ninth grade significantly increases students' chances of continuing on with mathematics study and succeeding in higher levels of mathematics in high school and college.[22] The role of algebra as a gatekeeper has divided students into classes with significantly different opportunities to learn. Currently, disproportionately high numbers of students of color are inadequately prepared in algebra and do not have access to serious mathematics beyond algebra in high school. Research on tracking[23] indicates that the reduced learning opportunities that characterize low-track mathematics classes often align with socioeconomic status and race. Little is known about the impact of policy decisions, such as requiring algebra of all students or including algebra in significant ways on high school exit examinations, on students from different backgrounds and on students of color. Even without answers to such crucial questions, policy decisions that have a direct impact on students' futures are being made daily.

The United States needs to take a close look at the issue of algebra learning in those segments of the population whose success rate in learning algebra has not been high. There are promising routes to algebra proficiency that seem effective within the social context of inner-city schools or schools that serve students of color—most notably, the efforts of Robert Moses and the Algebra Project. Research is needed to clarify how mathematics instruction can capitalize on the strengths that students from different cultural and linguistic groups bring to the classroom in order to enhance the learning of algebra. We know that education is resource dependent, and that communities of poverty often suffer from a lack of well-trained teachers, efficient administrators, and equipment that might support instruction. Some communities have developed strategies intended to address these problems so that their negative effect on students' learning can be reduced or eliminated; we need to examine these strategies through research that enables generalization and refinement of such strategies. The nation also needs a far better understanding of the ways in which policies, curriculum, and professional development opportunities lead teachers toward a heightened sense of accountability for the learning of algebra by all students.

---

[22]See Usiskin, 1995, and National Center for Education Statistics, 1994a, 1994b.

[23]Oakes, 1985, and Oakes, Gamoran & Page, 1992.

TOWARD A PARTNERSHIP BETWEEN GOVERNMENT AND THE MATHEMATICS EDUCATION RESEARCH COMMUNITY

Implementing the research and development program discussed in the previous three chapters will require forging a new partnership between the federal government and researchers and practitioners. Producing cumulative and usable knowledge related to mathematical proficiency and its equitable attainment will require the combined effort of mathematicians, researchers, developers, practitioners, and funding agencies. In this venture, the federal funding agencies, particularly the Office of Educational Research and Improvement (OERI), must take the lead. It is the leaders of the funding agencies who must make the case for the resources needed to implement the program described in this report. But beyond that, these funding agency leaders must also take the steps necessary to shape a funding and research and development infrastructure capable of carrying out this program.

In this chapter, we begin with some general observations about the qualities of the program that we envision. We then outline activities needed to carry out high-quality work that is strategic, cumulative, and useful. Finally, we suggest initial steps in creating the program.

THE NATURE OF THE PROPOSED PROGRAM OF RESEARCH AND DEVELOPMENT

The work proposed in this report fits into three broad classes of research and development activities:[1]

The first class comprises *descriptive studies* using appropriate and replicable methods to identify and define important aspects of mathematics learning and teaching. Such work would deal with key aspects of understanding and perfor-

---

[1] In framing these categories of activities, we drew heavily on concepts developed by the National Research Council Committee on Scientific Principles for Education Research (Shavelson & Towne, 2002). However, that committee did not extensively consider development, an important component of our third class of activities.

mance. Of interest would be changes in understanding and performance over time, associations and correlations across levels of schooling, and the connections among the phenomena of mathematics learning and instruction and the characteristics of students, teachers, and school systems. Studies in this area might include design experiments in which researchers actively create an intervention and study its effects in a specific setting. Taken together, such studies provide a basis for generating hypotheses, models, and theories about how mathematics learning and instruction work and about what might be done to improve it.

The second class of activities includes *research designed to develop and test models to explain the phenomena described in studies of the first type* using methods that support the attribution of causal relationships and allow identification of the processes and mechanisms that explain these causal relationships. These methods should deal appropriately and rigorously with the problem of ruling out alternative explanations for findings. This may be done through the use of experimental methods and randomization, but in cases where such methods are not feasible, researchers must pay careful attention to questions of how well their methods deal with potential threats to the validity of the conclusions drawn, given the particular purposes of the study.

The last class of work is *design and development* to produce knowledge, curricula, materials, tools, and tests that can actually be used in practice in particular situations. This design and development work ought to be based on the explanatory efforts and the hypotheses and theories identified and established in the first and second classes of activities. However, in most cases, such work will need to go beyond these two classes of research because the research will not be completely adequate to support the particular design. These design and development efforts should include appropriate and rigorous studies intended to establish whether or not the designs work, how well they work compared with other approaches, and the probability that they will work under specified conditions and in specified settings (including evidence on whether and how they work "at scale").

Such design and development work inevitably will generate problems, questions, and insights that will support, motivate, and inform work of the first two types. For example, an important line of research is the comparative study of different curriculum materials. Another is the design and comparison of alternative approaches to professional development.

The RAND Mathematics Study Panel advocates placing significant emphasis on this third class of activities. The creation of materials, tools, and processes that can be widely used in mathematics education is an important component of a problem-centered program of research and development. In fields such as medicine, agriculture, and computer science, this type of research-based development is key to advances in the technologies of each practice. For example, when a researcher discovers some molecular process in cell proteins, the public does not ask why practicing doctors are not utilizing the new knowledge. Instead, the vast public and private development infrastructure incorporates the new knowledge into its development programs. A new medicine or a new use of an existing treatment might result. At this point, when knowledge becomes a new technology, research can be directed to how doctors are using the new medicine and with what effect.

Such development programs in education will involve people with skills that are analogous to those of engineers in industrial sectors. The programs will typically also involve close collaboration with the users of the products—i.e., practitioners and policymakers. If properly carried out, these development efforts will also yield important insights concerning the scalability of interventions, the effects of various school contexts on the outcomes of an intervention, and requirements for effective implementation of a program or intervention. Some components of these development efforts may take the form of *problem-solving research and development* recently proposed by the National Academy of Education.[2]

Over time, OERI and other funders will need to consider the most appropriate means of supporting design and development. In other sectors of the economy, most development is carried out by the private rather than public sector. Increasingly, however, partnerships between researchers in universities and private profit-making and nonprofit organizations have become important. The proportion of the proposed program's resources devoted to research-based development will depend upon evolving decisions concerning the division of development responsibilities between the public and private sectors, as well as the promise of proposals for development. What we describe here represents a major change from the status quo of research enterprises in universities and research firms and will require the active support of program leadership.

A vital program of mathematics education research and development should include a variety of research and development activities. Figure 5.1 offers a schematic view of the proposed program's design. Some activities in each of the cells would be funded at the start of the program. Because each of the focal areas is important to the program's goals, we make no recommendation concerning the relative levels of funding for each of the areas. Instead, we expect those

---

[2]See National Academy of Education, 1999, and Sabelli & Dede, 2001.

RAND *MR1643-5.1*

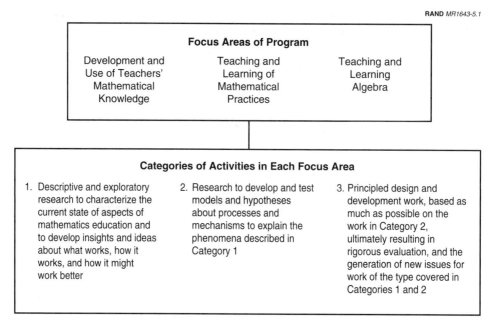

Figure 5.1—Components of the Proposed Mathematics Education Research and
Development Program

levels would be determined initially by the relative quality of the proposals submitted in the various areas.

However, as the program evolves through time, judgments will need to be made concerning the contributions that work in each area can make toward the goals of the program. Based on these judgments, funders will want to take actions to shape the balance of emphases in the program. Moreover, we expect that design and development (the third category of activities) will require increasing proportions of the total program funding as the program moves forward due to the cost of doing research-based development. In a subsequent section, we describe a mechanism for making judgments about the allocation of resources among these activities.

CRITERIA FOR THE QUALITY OF THE RESEARCH AND DEVELOPMENT PROGRAM

Articulating explicit criteria for the quality of the research and development program is important to ensure that the program meets high standards of rigor and usefulness. Criteria related to these standards would likely evolve as the program grows and changes. One set of criteria that appears crucial from the start deals with the selection, design, and conduct of program projects and initiatives. A second set of criteria concerns the kinds of communication, sharing, and critiquing vital to building high-quality knowledge-based and evidence-based resources for practice.[3]

With respect to the first set of criteria, the research and development program should *respond to pressing practical needs.* Improvement in the knowledge of mathematics for teaching, the teaching and learning of mathematical practices, and learning of algebra are all areas of practical need in which significant research questions can be investigated and research-based development efforts can be fruitful. Advanced mathematics is a gatekeeper in today's society, setting an entrance requirement for access to further education and economic opportunity while disproportionately creating barriers for students of color and students living in poverty. Thus, the research and development program should hold promise for promoting equitable practices in the teaching and learning of algebra.

In addition to being responsive to the needs of the practice community, the program should *build on existing research* wherever possible. The program should be cumulative, building on what is useful and proven and discarding lines of inquiry that have been shown to be unproductive.

An effective research and development program should also *be linked to relevant theory.* While a goal of research over the long term is to generate new knowledge, often in the form of new theories that provide explanatory and predictive power, scientific inquiry must be rooted in and guided by existing theoretical or conceptual frameworks. Development efforts should also be theoretically grounded. Although the goal of a principled design and development effort may be to create tools and program designs, theoretical or conceptual frames should drive the choices developers make—for example, in the inclusion and sequencing of particular algebraic concepts and skills in curriculum development. Similarly, researchers should use existing theories and conceptual frames as they make decisions about the types of evidence needed to support, refute, or refine their hypotheses.

To that end, the *methods a researcher uses should be appropriate for investigation of the chosen question* and reflect the theoretical stance taken. As Shavelson & Towne (2002) stated:

> Methods can only be judged in terms of their appropriateness and effectiveness in addressing a particular research question. Moreover, scientific claims are significantly strengthened when they are subject to testing by multiple methods. While appropriate methodology is important for individual studies, it also

---

[3]Again, in putting forth these criteria, we acknowledge our debt to the work of the NRC Committee on Scientific Principles in Education Research (Shavelson & Towne, 2002).

has a larger aspect. Particular research designs and methods are suited for specific kinds of investigations and questions, but can rarely illuminate all the questions and issues in a line of inquiry. Therefore, very different methodological approaches must often be used in various parts of a series of related studies.

A coordinated program of research and development would support groups of researchers to investigate significant questions from different theoretical and conceptual frames using methods consistent with both the questions and these frames.

A further criterion for a high-quality coordinated program of research and development is that the *findings of researchers and developers are regularly synthesized.* The use of common measures of independent and dependent variables across studies, where appropriate, will facilitate syntheses. The results of syntheses help to frame new research questions that seek to resolve inconsistent findings, address missing areas, replicate and generalize the results, and test interventions that are a result of research-based development. Synthesis work strengthens the validity of knowledge generated and enhances its usefulness and the usefulness of the products developed from that knowledge. To support syntheses, replication of results, and generalization of results to other settings, researchers and developers must *make their findings public and available for critique* through broad dissemination to appropriate research, development, and practice communities.

The program we envision would also support a *dynamic interchange between research and development* as progress in one area influences the other in a reciprocal fashion. Developers seeking to solve problems need to draw upon and, on occasion, carry out research to meet their objectives. Development, and the evaluation of development, will frequently raise questions that should be explored in new research.

In order to carefully scrutinize and critique the work of researchers and developers and begin to use the results of their work, the research and development community must have access to *an explicit and coherent explanation of the chains of reasoning that lead from empirical evidence to inferences.* A coordinated program of research and development requires detailed explanations of the procedures and methods of analysis used in collecting and examining empirical evidence. Additionally, developers should make explicit the evidence-based rationale for the choices made in development. This information should be available to the appropriate audiences, particularly the practitioners who use the products.

Developing a program possessing the qualities enumerated above would build a "culture of science" such as that recently described and advocated by the Committee on Scientific Principles for Education Research of the National Research Council. The RAND Mathematics Study Panel is aiming for a program characterized by such a culture coupled with an intimate connection with practice that facilitates effective use of the knowledge and other products produced by the program. The details of such a program are set forth in the next section.

AN ORGANIZATIONAL STRUCTURE TO CARRY OUT THE WORK

The criteria we discuss in the previous section strongly suggest that a coordinated, cumulative, and problem-centered program of research and development in mathematics would require skilled management and direction.[4] The focus on cumulativeness and rigor requires that government funders, as well as performers in the field, approach and manage their work differently than they have in the past. The exact nature of this management will evolve as the work unfolds and will depend on the size of the program.

The next several subsections describe a structure that might emerge over time. The structure consists of an overarching Mathematics Education Research Panel (which we discuss further at the end of this section) with support from three smaller Focus Area Panels for each of the three focus areas proposed in Chapters Two, Three, and Four. Finally, each focus area would ultimately be assisted by a Focus Area Center that would convene groups of researchers and practitioners concerned with the focal area, carry out periodic syntheses of work, and support both the government program offices and the panels.

Collectively, these efforts are intended to advance the cumulativeness and scientific quality of the program and promote the use of knowledge and products the program develops. The structure we propose is likely to be too elaborate for funding levels and activities in the initial year or two of the program. However, the description provides our sense of how a cooperative and coordinated program of research and development in mathematics education might be run as it gains size.

Focus Area Panels

One way in which the program might ultimately be organized is shown in Figure 5.2. We propose that the program be organized according to the three focus

---

[4]As of this writing, OERI is in the process of being reauthorized, and its organization is likely to change. Moreover, there appears to be increasing use of joint programs, such as the Interagency Education Research Initiative that coordinates funding from OERI, National Science Foundation, and National Institutes of Health, in an effort to capitalize on the strengths of each agency. The organization proposal suggested in this chapter, which is based on the current OERI structure, would need to be tailored to future organizational and funding situations.

areas that the RAND panel has identified. For each focus area, a standing panel would be created. These panels would have three important roles. They would (1) advise OERI and other funders on priorities and guidance to be included in Requests for Applications, as well as (2) suggest criteria by which to judge the quality of proposals and provide recommendations for expert peer reviewers to OERI and other funders. Periodically, the panels also would (3) analyze and interpret the yield of the work in the focus areas and carry out planning exercises extending and revising the plans that exist for each focus area. Their work would be advisory. OERI and other funding agencies would manage the actual peer review of proposals.

The panels shown in Figure 5.2 constitute a major means for fostering the co-ordinated action proposed in this report. The government would appoint the panels, and their members would have staggered terms in order to promote continuity. The membership of the panels should represent a wide range of viewpoints, including those of mathematics education researchers, mathematicians, mathematics educators, cognitive scientists, developer/engineers, experts in measurement, and policymakers. As we note later in this chapter, each panel will be assisted in its work by a Focus Area Center.

RAND *MR1643-5.2*

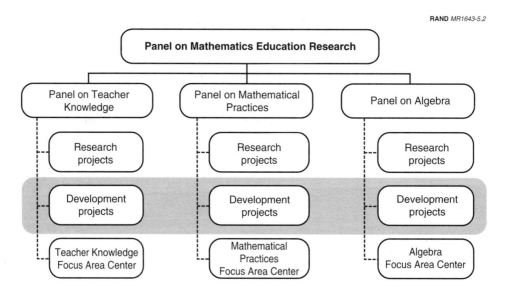

Figure 5.2—Major Activities in the Proposed Mathematics Education Research and Development Program

Activities in Each Focus Area

The trio of boxes under each panel box in Figure 5.2 denotes the major classes of activities within the program. The meaning of the top two is obvious; they are the research and development projects that make up the program. (The shaded area indicates that development projects often cross over focus areas.) The third class of activity, located in the Focus Area Centers, involves a number of functions to promote and support this cooperative and coordinated research and development effort. For example, a center would carry out periodic research syntheses. It would convene leaders of funded research and development projects to discuss ongoing work and crosscutting and comparative results. It might serve as a means for coordinating the development of common measures to foster the comparison of research findings and replication of research results. Finally, a center might provide various "contracted out" functions in support of OERI's management of the program.

The Focus Area Centers would be jointly supervised by the appropriate Focus Area Panel and personnel from the funding agencies. The centers would be selected on the basis of a targeted competition.

The Role of the Panel on Mathematics Education Research

As the program evolves, it will be important to carry out efforts seeking to make collective sense out of the work being supported in the various focus areas. We propose that this function be the responsibility of a Panel on Mathematics Education Research. In carrying out its duties, this comprehensive panel would work closely with the Focus Area Panels under it and the Focus Area Panels' respective centers. If sufficient resources become available, the panel might propose additional focus areas that should be added to the work being carried out in the three focus areas. It might also propose research-based development programs that span the focus areas. The Panel on Mathematics Education Research would advise OERI and other funders concerning improved policies relating to the management of the program and ways to promote effective use of the results of the program's work. Finally, as with any research and development enterprise, carrying out a comprehensive program review every three to five years is imperative. This would be a responsibility of the Panel on Mathematics Education Research.

Whereas the RAND Mathematics Study Panel proposes that the Focus Area Panels be made up largely of individuals with expertise in research, development, or practice, the Panel on Mathematics Education Research should have a broader membership. While we recommend the panel have strong representation from the research community, its membership should also include policymakers, members of the business and professional communities, and others with a strong concern for the quality of mathematics education. As with the Focus Area Panels, this panel would be appointed by and advise OERI. The Panel on Mathematics Education Research, with support from the Focus Area Centers, should publish a biennial report on the progress of the program.[5]

THE ROLE OF OERI IN CONDUCTING PRACTICE-CENTERED RESEARCH AND DEVELOPMENT

As of this writing, Congress is considering the reauthorization of OERI. The exact form of the reauthorized agency is unknown, but it seems clear that many members of Congress seek a stronger and more rigorous program of education research that embodies the features of good science. The RAND Mathematics Study Panel strongly supports such a goal. Our suggestions concerning OERI's role in the program are motivated by this goal.

In mounting a program of mathematics education research and development, OERI and its successor agency have several crucial roles to play. In particular, they should:

- Provide active overall leadership for the mathematics education research and development program

- Manage the processes of solicitation and selection of research and development projects and programs in a way that promotes work of high scientific quality and usefulness consistent with the principles outlined in this chapter

- Work in ways that build both the quality and extent of the infrastructure within which the research and development in mathematics education are carried out.

We treat each of these roles briefly in turn.

Leadership

Perhaps the most critical function that OERI must play is to provide leadership to the collective effort proposed in this report. Although we have recommended a set of panels to advise and assist OERI, panels are seldom able to lead. Pro-

---

[5]The pending reauthorization of OERI may well make new provisions for an advisory and/or governing board for the agency. It is conceivable that the substantive review and planning of the agency's high-priority research and development, which we suggest should be assigned to a Panel on Mathematics Education Research, could instead be assigned to a subcommittee of such a panel (which presumably would also have business, professional, and policymaker representation). It would be important to avoid unnecessary duplication of these functions.

gram managers (and supporting staff) are needed who are willing and able to make decisions concerning program strategy, create a culture within OERI emphasizing excellence in research and development, and represent the program to superiors in government and to Congress. They should have both the capability and the time to be substantively involved with the work of the program. The leaders should be able to gain the confidence of and work with both researchers and educators. Our panel's view on this echoes that of the National Research Council's Committee on Scientific Principles for Education Research, whose first design principle for fostering high-qualitative scientific work in a federal education research agency is to "staff the agency with people skilled in science, leadership, and management."[6]

Historically, it has been difficult to recruit such staff to OERI. In part, this difficulty reflects the agency's reputation as a place where it is difficult to do good work. Probably more important is the fact that the agency had little funding to carry out work of the scope and quality that the RAND panel is proposing. We recommend that the leadership of OERI make explicit efforts to create positions and working conditions that will be attractive to the kinds of people capable of leading and managing the program we propose. But OERI cannot do this by itself. Senior people in the mathematics education research field have an obligation to help OERI by encouraging their talented junior colleagues to spend time in OERI and by supporting the OERI staff through active and constructive participation in the peer review and advisory processes.

Managing for High Scientific Quality and Usefulness

A cornerstone of good management in a research and development funding agency is an effective process for ensuring the quality of the work that is supported. Creating an effective peer review system that involves individuals with high levels of expertise in the subjects and research methods of concern is crucial. A peer review system that has the confidence of the field and of the scientific community is likely to attract high-quality researchers and provide reasonable assurance that quality proposals are supported. While the RAND panel advocates a system for effective peer review that possesses some continuity in the reviewers from funding cycle to funding cycle, we have not examined the administrative requirements of OERI in sufficient detail to recommend specifics concerning the management of the peer review system.

The Panel on Mathematics Education Research and the three focus area panels that we propose are not intended to be part of the peer review process in the selection of proposals. Individual members of these panels might serve as peer

---

[6]Shavelson & Towne, 2002, p. 7.

reviewers. However, these standing panels do have important roles to play in the quality assurance process. In their role of synthesizing the research, they will have the opportunity to review the quality of the work that has been supported by the program and advise OERI concerning this quality.

The Focus Area Panels also play another potential role in promoting the scientific quality of the program. They should identify areas where replication of research findings should be sought or where work examining possible alternative explanations for research findings should be encouraged. In short, the panels could play an important role in creating the culture of scientific inquiry that is necessary to the success of the program.

Finally, OERI should emulate the National Institutes of Health (NIH) and parts of the National Science Foundation (NSF) in using the results of peer reviews to help unsuccessful applicants for grants to improve and resubmit proposals that are worthy of support. Working with the applicants is another way in which the OERI program staff can be substantively involved with the program and in which peer review can be used to improve the quality of work in the program.

Concern for Enhancing the Research and Development Infrastructure

We agree with the National Research Council's Committee on Scientific Principles for Education Research that investment in the research infrastructure will be an important contributor to the quality of an effective program of research and development.[7] We go beyond that committee's recommendations to emphasize the importance of an infrastructure that supports the research-based development and scaling of research findings that we see as being important to the improvement of practice.

OERI can enhance the infrastructure for research and development in a number of ways:

- As an early step in developing a mathematics education research and development program, OERI should consider a special effort to assemble and, where necessary, develop measurement instruments and technology that could be widely used by researchers, and thus enhance the opportunities for comparing and contrasting findings of various research efforts.

- OERI should be prepared to create or enhance institutions for carrying out mathematics education research and development where a clear need and function can be demonstrated. The commissioning of the Focus Area Centers suggested earlier would be an example of such institution building.

---

[7]Shavelson & Towne, 2002.

- OERI solicitations associated with a mathematics education research and development program should include encouragement for the training and mentoring of young scholars as a means of attracting new people to the field.

Communications among researchers in the field should be enhanced through the activities of the proposed panels. In producing this report, for example, the widespread review and discussion of the first draft was invaluable. Open discussion and critique contribute to the development of the field. Advancement of science depends on open debate unconstrained by orthodoxies and political agendas. To promote this discussion and critique, the composition of the panels and the extended research communities must include individuals with critical perspectives.

While these suggestions are specific, they are part of a more general recommendation that OERI should take responsibility for developing an infrastructure that will improve the quality of research and development in mathematics education and strengthen the research field's capacity to engage in high-quality work.

INITIAL STEPS IN IMPLEMENTING THE PROPOSED PROGRAM

The proposed program is ambitious and strategic. Based on hypotheses about the areas in which investments will yield high payoffs for increasing the mathematical proficiency of all students, the program places great value on scientific rigor and the usability of the knowledge produced. However, the recommendations will bear fruit only if the president and Congress are willing to significantly increase the level of spending on mathematics research and development. Assuming that a promise of such funding exists, where should OERI start?

The RAND panel recommends that a mathematics education research and development program begin with two important efforts:

- A research solicitation structured around the three focus areas discussed above

- Several targeted research efforts to examine the current state of mathematics instruction in K–12 schools, with the intent of providing clearer direction for future research and development.

If sufficient resources are available, an early solicitation might also seek proposals for research-based development work in areas in which there is sufficiently promising theory to justify the investment.

The first of the two initiatives would signal the intent to support a solid and rigorous program of research in the three focus areas. The solicitation would seek proposals for work that builds on what is known, clearly specifies the research questions to be addressed, and uses methodologies appropriate to those questions. The results of the initial solicitation should provide important input to OERI and the proposed panels as they strive to build a cumulative and high-quality program of research and development.

The second component of the initial program effort would be somewhat more directed than the first. As we discussed in this report's introduction, mathematics education is a subject of considerable controversy. Claims and counterclaims abound concerning the value of various curricular strategies and curricula, requirements for teacher knowledge, and standards that students should meet. For the most part, these debates are poorly informed by solid research due to the dearth of such research. The program proposed in this report is most likely to gain the political support necessary for its success if it begins with activities designed to reshape these debates into empirically based investigations of the issues that underlie competing claims.

In this regard, we propose three classes of studies:

- Studies providing empirical input on the necessarily political decisions concerning standards of mathematical proficiency that students must meet

- Research intended to create a systematic picture of the nature of current mathematics education in the nation's classrooms

- Studies that assemble existing measures of mathematical performance or develop new ones that can be used throughout the proposed program.

The details of such studies should be developed by OERI and other funders working with research experts and educators from the field.

We illustrate the sorts of studies that might be done in the brief descriptions in the two text boxes that follow. The nature of these studies implies that further development of collective and collaborative efforts, such as those associated with The Third International Mathematics and Science Study (TIMSS), needs to be done. The studies exemplify some features of the collaboration among funders, researchers, and practitioners that we have recommended.

Research Related to Standards for Proficiency to Be Achieved by Students

One of the contentious areas in mathematics education is the standard that students should be expected to achieve and that the schools should be expected to enable students to achieve. Setting such standards is a political task rather than a research task. Nonetheless, empirical research on the needs of adults in the United States for proficiency in various areas of mathematics could help political bodies as they set such standards. Empirical research on the effects of current standards in specific communities could reveal the consequences of various formats and specifications of standards on the development of student proficiency. A matter of particular concern is the (often unanticipated) impacts that various specifications of standards have on diverse groups of students.

Research on the Nature of Current Mathematics Education in the Nation's Classrooms

While there is active and vigorous debate about the nature of the mathematics curricula that should be used in the nation's schools and the knowledge that is necessary for a teacher to be effective with those curricula, surprisingly little systematic knowledge exists about the actual implementation and use of programs and materials. Much of the evidence cited in these debates relies on anecdotes and firsthand experience. And the data used in these debates lack rigor, both in the nature of the information gathered and in the methods used

---

Example of Research on Existing Mathematics Curricular Materials

A possible starting point for examining the current practices in mathematics education would be to support systematic research on the quality and use of currently existing mathematics curricular materials. Some of these materials have been developed with support from the National Science Foundation, which expected that the developers would draw on the existing research base. Other materials are commercially developed and may or may not be research based. Some curricular materials are advanced by one side of the math wars and others by the other side. A coordinated program of research on mathematics curricula might, for example, have a middle school focus and ask:

- How do these materials deal with algebra?
- Who is using each of the various curricula, what is the extent of use, and what is the type of use?
- How distinct are these curricula in the algebraic content they cover?
- How well are the curricula implemented—are some easier than others to use appropriately by a broad range of teachers?
- What is the teacher knowledge implied by each curriculum, and how are middle school teachers distributed against that required knowledge base?
- What are the effects on gains in student achievement?
- How does the level of implementation, type of student, and knowledge of teachers explain these effects?

to analyze that information. For example, test score data are often used with little attention paid to the differences in student populations, the nature of the teaching staff, the levels of student mobility, or the character of the implementation of various programs.

One of the early initiatives in a program of mathematics education research and development should be a collaborative national effort to develop a systematic and empirical understanding of the actual nature of current mathematics education in U.S. schools. The goal of this part of the research and development effort would be to provide a grounded empirical base for policy concerning mathematics education and to provide a better understanding upon which to design improvement efforts.

Existing research efforts can provide some guidance and a base upon which to build further efforts. The TIMSS that compared mathematics performance internationally contains information on the nature of curriculum and instruction, and there is some limited information on curriculum and instruction in the

---

Example of Research on Existing Mathematical Knowledge of Teachers of Mathematics and Its Impact on Mathematics Instruction

Research has begun to uncover more about the role that mathematics knowledge plays in effective teaching. An initial program of research might build on this recent progress by focusing on the knowledge that teachers need to teach algebra at different levels. Questions include:

- What do teachers know of algebra and the skills and language related to the use and teaching of algebra? How does this compare across grade levels—elementary, middle, and high school?

- Are there recurrent mathematical issues that arise in the course of teaching algebra that demand specific teacher knowledge? In other words, are there some priority or high-leverage areas of knowledge for teaching algebra?

- In what ways does teachers' knowledge impact the quality of their teaching? What relations exist between particular types of teacher knowledge and their instructional patterns, and, in turn, their students' learning?

- What do different curricula demand of teachers?

- Are there types of curricula/programs (including technology) that can diminish the strength of the relationships between teacher content knowledge and student learning (i.e., support for teachers that enables them to be successful even when mathematical knowledge is lacking)?

A program of research on teacher content knowledge would require continued development of instruments to assess teacher knowledge. In the long run, we believe that measures of teacher content knowledge should be routinely included in all research studies of mathematics education.

National Assessment of Educational Progress. But much more needs to be done to create a national effort that engages excellent researchers and produces studies that build knowledge cumulatively. A significant design effort also would be required. Common measurement instruments would need to be designed or adopted and adapted. And, finally, a structure to manage the overall effort would need to be developed.

An effort such as this has several goals. The studies would establish a baseline against which changes and improvement (or lack of improvement) can be measured. They would describe the complex array of factors that determine the achieved mathematics proficiency of students. By going beyond single-factor explanations of effects, these studies would contribute to the development of more realistic designs for programs meant to improve the mathematical proficiency of all students.

Studies on the Development of Improved Measures of Mathematical Performance

The final activity that should be started early in the program is the development of measures and measurement instruments that can be used widely by those conducting the research on mathematics education. Without common and agreed-upon measures that permit comparisons of the study results of distinctive instructional programs or of similar programs in different settings, there will be an inadequate basis for building the rigorous program of research and development outlined in this report. Wide participation of the research community in the development of measures will be needed, and funders should be willing to specify where common measures must be used to promote the cumulative and scientific character of the program.

FUNDING RESOURCES

We made no attempt to estimate the cost of a program such as the one we propose. Obviously, meeting the program goals envisioned here will demand a significant investment of resources. The emphasis placed on enhancing the scientific rigor of the effort through the use of appropriate methods, replication of results, and wider use of experimental designs in tests of theories and hypotheses will require substantial support, and such work demands resources. Moreover, for new knowledge to find wide use in the classroom, it will need to be embodied in the curricula, materials, tools, and activities that themselves will require design, testing, redesign, retesting, and, ultimately, rigorous validation through solid research. This process, too, is expensive.

During the course of this study effort, we attempted to estimate the amount of resources that have been devoted to mathematics education research, excluding development. Including both NSF and OERI funding, the investment was estimated to be about $20 million annually between fiscal year (FY) 1996 and FY 2001. In FY 2002, NSF made significant commitments to a series of mathematics and science partnerships between universities and selected communities that will involve some research and development. Still, the funding is modest. By contrast, the early-reading research programs at NIH are currently funded at a level of more than $50 million annually in direct costs, also without much support going to development.

The program proposed here, particularly if it is to embody the work necessary to achieve high scientific rigor, clearly will require major increments in funding of mathematics education research.

Chapter Six

CONCLUSIONS

The United States needs to improve the mathematical proficiency of all students in the nation's schools. The personal, occupational, and educational demands placed on all Americans in the 21st century call for a level of mathematical proficiency that in generations past was required of only a few. Moreover, as both a moral imperative and a matter of national interest, the nation should move to reduce the gaps in mathematics proficiency that now exist between the economically advantaged and the disadvantaged and among the diverse groups that populate the nation.

However, the U.S. educational system faces serious problems that impede the attainment of these goals. Many students are taught by teachers who are under-prepared to teach mathematics, and those poorly prepared teachers are disproportionately working with students from less-advantaged backgrounds and students of color. Useful mathematics curricula and mathematics education programs exist, but they are weakly implemented in many, if not most, American schools. Teacher development programs to help teachers achieve the required professional skills are uneven in quality, and too often those who need these programs the most do not participate in them. Nevertheless, the research, education, and education policy communities now have the knowledge and resources to make significant progress in mathematics proficiency. The nation can and must do better with the knowledge and resources it already has.

The message of this report by the RAND Mathematics Study Panel is that the research and education communities need to know more and do much more if the nation is to achieve adequate levels of mathematical proficiency for all students. The research and education communities need to identify the knowledge that can enable teachers to help their students develop mathematical proficiency, and they need to develop robust ways of helping teachers acquire and use that knowledge. The research and education communities also need to learn how children, who bring different personal experiences to school with them, learn the mathematical practices that are essential to effective day-to-day use of mathematics. Moreover, we argue that algebra, and more generally the broad mathematical skills that algebra encompasses, are critical both to mathematical proficiency and to equity in the achievement of proficiency.

To provide the necessary knowledge *and* the capacity to use that knowledge in practice, this report recommends a significant program of research and development aimed at building resources for improved teaching and learning. Because resources are limited, the panel deliberated at length to identify the research areas that are most likely to yield improved knowledge and practice and to attain the dual goals of mathematical proficiency and equity in the acquisition of proficiency.

This report recommends three priority focus areas for programmatic research and development—developing teachers' mathematical knowledge in ways that are directly useful for teaching, teaching and learning skills for mathematical thinking and problem solving, and teaching and learning of algebra from kindergarten through 12th grade. These research areas, and the reasons for their selection, are discussed in Chapters Two through Four of this report.

The RAND panel has also made proposals on how the research and development program should be conducted. New approaches to program funding and new management styles are recommended. These approaches should ensure that the supported work incorporates effective scientific practices, uses methods appropriate to the goals of the component projects, and that the program builds knowledge over time. Further, interventions should be rigorously tested and revised through cycles of design and trial.

The program we propose will require contributions of individuals with wide-ranging skills and sustained commitment on the part of the federal offices that support research and development in mathematics education. The staff in these offices must be adept at engaging the research and education communities in the partnership that we have argued is necessary to move forward with the program we propose. Federal office staff must organize the program in ways that ensure the rigor, cumulativeness, and usability of the research and development. They must bring outstanding individuals into the planning of the work and into the selection of the proposals, people, and institutions that can carry it out most effectively. They must arrange for the regular critical review and evaluation of what has been supported and what has been learned, and they must make adjustments in the program that are suggested by such review.

However, the necessary changes extend beyond the funding agencies. The research community concerned with mathematics education must change as well. Perhaps because mathematics education research has been so poorly funded in the past, too much of the research has taken place with relatively small projects, has used diverse methods that can make the results difficult to compare, and has, therefore, yielded too little knowledge that is cumulative and usable. The agenda that we propose in this report will require greater collaboration and interdisciplinary action in planning, more willingness on the part of researchers to do the work necessary to develop and use common measures, and more attention paid to working collectively to build both knowledge and practice.

Moreover, both funders and researchers must develop better ways to engage the practitioner community in this work. It is not enough to have a single practitioner serving as a member of a peer review group or serving on a study panel. Research and development initiatives must be more solidly informed and guided by the wisdom of practice. New institutions that can engage researchers and practitioners in joint work are needed. New partnerships between research institutions and schools and school districts must be forged. The research and development program that the RAND panel proposes is unlikely to produce usable results if progress is not made in bridging research and practice.

While some issues surrounding mathematics education, particularly concerning what it is that students should know and be able to do in mathematics, involve inherently political decisions, we believe that most of these issues can be illuminated by appropriate and timely research and evaluation. Current debates surrounding mathematics education have not been adequately informed by the work of the research community. Because of this, these debates have often been undisciplined and overly contentious. The program of research and development envisioned in this report is intended to move the nation beyond these debates to significant improvements in student learning.

Achieving what we envision will require building and enhancing a vigorous and critical research, development, and practice community. Within such a community, we hope that debate among those with varying and competing views concerning standards of proficiency, curricular designs, pedagogical styles, and assessment methods will evolve into a discourse that is based less on ideology and more on evidence.

The RAND Mathematics Study Panel asserts that our nation's future well-being depends on shifts in how research and development in mathematics education are designed, supported, coordinated, and managed. Mathematical proficiency is one of the most important capabilities needed by the people of the United States in the 21st century. Achieving mathematical proficiency equitably will require the targeted investment recommended in this report.

Abt Associates. (1993). Prospects: The congressionally mandated study of educational growth and opportunity. Cambridge, Mass.: Abt Associates.

Achieve. (2002). Foundations for success: Mathematics expectations for the middle grades (consultation draft). Washington, DC: National Academy Press.

Aguirre, J. (2002). Moving beyond curriculum reform: Negotiating tensions between collective responsibility and professional autonomy as conditions for teacher learning in math departments. Paper presented at the Annual Meeting of the American Educational Research Association, New Orleans, LA.

Anyon, J. (1981). Social class and school knowledge. Curriculum Inquiry, 11(1), 3–42.

Atweh, B., Bleicher, R. E., & Cooper, T. J. (1998). The construction of the social context of mathematics classrooms: A sociolinguistic analysis. Journal for Research in Mathematics Education, (29)1, 63–82.

Balacheff, N. (1988). Aspects of proof in pupils' practice of school mathematics. In D. Pimm (Ed.), Mathematics, teachers, and children (pp. 216–230). London: Hodder & Stoughton.

Banchoff, T. (Ed.). (1988). ECM/87: Educational computing in mathematics. Proceedings of the International Congress on Educational Computing in Mathematics, Rome, Italy, June, 4–6, 1987. Amsterdam: North Holland.

Barnett, C. S. (1991). Building a case-based curriculum to enhance the pedagogical content knowledge of mathematics teachers. Journal of Teacher Education, 42, 263–272.

Barnett, C. S., Goldenstein, D., Jackson, B., & Bertauski, N. A. (1994). Fractions, decimals, ratios, and percents: Hard to teach and hard to learn? Portsmouth, NH: Heinemann.

Bednarz, N., Kieran, C., & Lee, L. (Eds.). (1996). Approaches to algebra: Perspectives for research and teaching. Dordrecht, Netherlands: Kluwer Academic Publishers.

Begle, E. G. (1979). The goals of mathematics education. In critical variables in mathematics education: Findings from a survey of the empirical literature. Washington, DC: Mathematics Association of America/National Council of Teachers of Mathematics.

Bell, A. (1976). A study of pupils' proof-explanations in mathematical situations. Educational Studies in Mathematics, 7, 23–40.

Blum, W., & Kirsch, A. (1991). Preformal proving: Examples and reflections. Educational Studies in Mathematics, 22(2), 183–203.

Boaler, J. (2002). Experiencing school mathematics: Traditional and reform approaches to teaching and their impact on student learning. Mahwah, NJ: Lawrence Erlbaum Associates.

Booth, L. (1984). Algebra: Children's strategies and errors. Windsor, UK: NFER-Nelson.

Borko, H., Eisenhart, M., & Brown, C. (1992). Learning to teach hard mathematics: Do novice teachers and their instructors give up too easily? Journal for Research in Mathematics Education, 23, 194–222.

Borko, H., & Putnam, R. (1996). Learning to teach. In D. Berliner & R. Calfee (Eds.), Handbook of educational psychology (pp. 673–708). New York, NY: Macmillan.

Braswell, J. S., Lutkus, A. D., Grigg, W. S., Santapau, S. L., Tay-Lim, B., & Johnson, M. (2001). The nation's report card: Mathematics 2000. Washington, DC: National Center for Educational Statistics.

Carpenter, T. P., Fennema, E., & Franke, M. L. (1996). Cognitively guided instruction: A knowledge base for reform in primary mathematics instruction. The Elementary School Journal, 97(1), 3–20.

Carpenter, T. P., Fennema, E., Peterson, P. L., Chiang, C. P., & Loef, M. (1989). Using knowledge of children's mathematics thinking in classroom teaching: An experimental study. American Educational Research Journal, 26(4), 499–531.

Carpenter, T. P., & Levi, L. (April 1999). Developing conceptions of algebraic reasoning in the primary grades. Paper presented at the annual meeting of the American Educational Research Association, Montreal, Canada.

Charles, R., & Silver, E. A. (Eds.). (1989). Teaching and assessing of mathematical problem solving. Mahwah, NJ: Lawrence Erlbaum Associates.

Chazan, D. (1993). High school geometry students' justification for their views of empirical evidence and mathematical proof. Educational Studies in Mathematics, 24(4), 359–387.

Chazan, D. (2000). Beyond formulas in mathematics and teaching: Dynamics of the high school algebra classroom. New York, NY: Teachers College Press.

Civil, M. (2002). Everyday mathematics, mathematicians' mathematics, and school mathematics: Can we bring them together? In M. Brenner and J. Moschkovich (Eds.), Everyday and academic mathematics in the classroom. Journal of Research in Mathematics Education, Monograph 11, 40–62. Reston, VA: NCTM.

Cobb, P., Wood, T. L., & Yackel, E. (1991). Assessment of a problem-centered second-grade mathematics project. Journal for Research in Mathematics Education, 22, 3–29.

Coe, R., & Ruthven, K. (1994). Proof practices and constructs of advanced mathematics students. British Educational Research Journal, 2(1), 41–53.

Cohen, D. K., & Hill, H. C. (2000). Instructional policy and classroom performance: The mathematics reform in California, Teachers College Record, 102(2), 294–343.

Collis, K. (1975). The development of formal reasoning. Newcastle, Australia: University of Newcastle.

Conference Board of the Mathematical Sciences. (2001). The mathematical education of teachers. Washington, DC: Conference Board of the Mathematical Sciences.

Council of Great City Schools. (2000). The urban teacher challenge: Teacher demand in the great city schools (pp. 9–11). Washington, DC: Council of Great City Schools.

Darling-Hammond, L. (1994). Teacher quality and equality. In J. I. Goodlad & P. Keating (Eds.), Access to knowledge: The continuing agenda for our nations' schools. New York, NY: College Entrance Examination Board.

De Villiers, M. (1990). The role and function of proof in mathematics. Pythagoras, 24, 17–24.

Devlin, K. J. (1999). Mathematics: The new golden age. New York, NY: Columbia University Press.

DiSessa, A. A., Hammer, D., Sherin, B., & Kolpakowski, T. (1991). Inventing graphing: Meta-representational expertise in children. Journal of Mathematical Behavior, 10, 117–160.

Dreyfus, T., & Hadas, N. (1996). Proof as an answer to the question why. Zentralblatt für Didaktik der Mathematik (International Reviews on Mathematical Education), 96(1), 1–5.

Dubinsky, E., & Harel, G. (1992). The nature of the process of conception of function. In G. Harel & E. Dubinsky (Eds.), The concept of function: Aspects of epistemology and pedagogy (MAA Notes, 25, pp. 85–106). Washington, DC: Mathematical Association of America.

Eisenhart, M., Borko, H., & Underhill, R. (1993). Conceptual knowledge falls through the cracks: Complexities of learning to teach mathematics for understanding. Journal for Research in Mathematics Education, 24, 8–40.

Even, R. (1990). Subject matter knowledge for teaching and the case of functions. Educational Studies in Mathematics, 21(6), 521–524.

Even, R. (1998). Factors involved in linking representations of functions. Journal of Mathematical Behavior, 17(1), 105–121.

Ferguson, R. (1991). Paying for public education: New evidence on how and why money matters. Harvard Journal of Legislation, 28, 465–498.

Ferrini-Mundy, J., Lappan, G., & Phillips, E. (1996). Experiences with algebraic thinking in the elementary grades: Teaching children mathematics. Reston, VA: National Council of Teachers of Mathematics.

Gallardo, A. (2001). Historical-epistemological analysis in mathematics education: Two works in didactics of algebra. In R. Sutherland, T. Rojano, & R. Lins (Eds.), Perspectives on school algebra. Dordrecht, Netherlands: Kluwer Academic Publishers.

Gamoran, A., Porter, A. C., Smithson, J., & Whith, P. A. (1997). Upgrading high school mathematics instruction: Improving learning opportunities for low-achieving, low-income youth. Educational Evaluation and Policy Analysis, 19(4), 325–338.

Garet, M., Porter, A., Desimone, L., Birman, B., & Yoon, K. (2001). What makes professional development effective: Results from a national sample of teachers. American Educational Research Journal, 38(4), 915–945.

Goldin, G. A. (1998). Representational systems, learning, and problem solving in mathematics. Journal of Mathematical Behavior, 17(2), 137–165.

Goldin, G. A., & McClintock, C. E. (Eds.). (1984). Task variables in mathematical problem solving. Philadelphia, PA: Franklin Institute Press (acquired by Lawrence Erlbaum Associates in Hillsdale, NJ).

Graeber, A., & Tirosh, D. (1991). The effect of problem type and common misconceptions on preservice elementary teachers' thinking about division. School Science and Mathematics, 91, 157–164.

Gutiérrez, R. (1996). Practices, beliefs, and cultures of high school mathematics departments: Understanding their influence on student achievement. Journal of Curriculum Studies, 28, 495–529.

Gutiérrez, R. (2002a). Beyond essentialism: The complexity of language in teaching mathematics to Latina/o students. American Educational Research Journal, 39(4).

Gutiérrez, R. (2002b). Enabling the practice of mathematics teachers in context: Toward a new equity research agenda. Mathematical Thinking and Learning, 4(2/3), 145–187.

Haberman, M. (1991). The pedagogy of poverty versus good teaching. Phi Delta Kappan, 73, 290–294.

Hall, R., & Stevens, R. (1995). Making space: A comparison of mathematical work in school and professional design practices. In S. L. Star (Ed.), The cultures of computing (pp. 118–145). London, UK: Basil Blackwell.

Hanna, G., & Jahnke, H. N. (1996). Proof and proving. In A. Bishop, K. Clements, C. Keitel, J. Kilpatrick, & C. Laborde (Eds.), International handbook of mathematics education (pp. 877–908). Dordrecht, Netherlands: Kluwer Academic Publishers.

Harel, G., & Dubinsky, E. (1992). The concept of function: Aspects of epistemology and pedagogy. MAA Notes, 25.

Heid, K. (1996). A technology-intensive functional approach to the emergence of algebraic thinking. In N. Bednarz, C. Kieran & L. Lee (Eds.), Approaches to Algebra: Perspectives for research and teaching (pp. 239–255). Dordrecht, Netherlands: Kluwer Academic Publishers.

Heid, K. (1997). The technological revolution and the reform of school mathematics. American Journal of Education, 106(1), 5–61.

Hiebert, J., Carpenter, T. P., Fennema, E., Fuson, K., Human, P., Murray, H., Olivier, A., & Wearne, D. (1997). Making sense: Teaching and learning mathematics with understanding. Portsmouth, NH: Heinemann.

Hoyles, C., Noss, R., & Pozzi, S. (2001). Proportional reasoning in nursing practice. Journal for Research in Mathematics Education, 32(1), 4–27.

Janvier, C. (Ed.). (1987). Problems of representation in the teaching and learning of mathematics. Hillsdale, NJ: Lawrence Erlbaum Associates.

Kaput, J. J. (1998a). Representations, inscriptions, descriptions and learning: A kaleidoscope of windows. Journal of Mathematical Behavior 17(2), 265–281.

Kaput, J. J. (1998b). Transforming algebra from an engine of inequity to an engine of mathematical power by "algebrafying" the K–12 curriculum. In National Council of Teachers of Mathematics and the Mathematical Sciences Education Board, National Research Council, The nature and role of algebra in the K–14 curriculum. Washington, DC: National Academy Press.

Kennedy, M. (1997). Defining optimal knowledge for teaching science and mathematics (Research Monograph 10). Madison, WI: National Institute for Science Education, University of Wisconsin,

Kenney, P. A., & Silver, E. A. (Eds.). (1997). Results from the Sixth Mathematics Assessment of the National Assessment of Educational Progress. Reston, VA: National Council of Teachers of Mathematics.

Khisty, L. L. (1997). Making mathematics accessible to Latino students: Rethinking instructional practice. In J. Trentacosta (Ed.), Multicultural and gender equity in the mathematics classroom: The gift of diversity (pp. 92–101). Reston, VA: National Council of Teachers of Mathematics.

Kieran, C. (1981). Concepts associated with the equality symbol. Educational Studies in Mathematics, 12, 317–326.

Kieran C. (1992). The learning and teaching of school algebra. In D. A. Grouws (Ed.) Handbook of research on mathematics teaching and learning (pp. 390–419). New York, NY: Macmillan.

Kilpatrick, J., Swafford, J., & Findell, B. (Eds.). (2001). Adding it up: Helping children learn mathematics. Washington, DC: National Academy Press.

Kuchemann, D. (1981). Algebra. In K. Hart (Ed.), Children's understanding of mathematics: 11–16 (pp. 102–119). London, UK: John Murray.

Lacampagne, C., Blair, W., & Kaput, J. (Eds.). (1995). The algebra initiative colloquium. Washington, DC: U.S. Department of Education.

Lappan, G., Fey, J., Fitzgerald, W., Friel, S., & Phillips, E. (1998). Say it with symbols: Algebraic reasoning, connected mathematics algebra. Menlo Park, CA: Dale Seymour Publications.

Lave, J. (1988). Cognition in practice: Mind, mathematics, and culture in everyday life. New York, NY: Cambridge University Press.

Learning First Alliance. (1998). Every child mathematically proficient: An action plan. Washington, DC: Learning First Alliance (www.learningfirst.org).

Lee, C., & Majors, Y. (2000). Cultural modeling's response to Rogoff's challenge: Understanding apprenticeship, guided participation, and participatory appropriation in a culturally responsive, subject-matter specific context. Paper presented at the annual meeting of the American Educational Research Association, New Orleans, LA.

Lee, V. E., with Smith, J. B. (forthcoming). High school restructuring and student achievement (. New York, NY: Teachers College Press.

Leinhardt, G., Zaslavsky, O., & Stein, M. (1990). Functions, graphs, and graphing: Tasks, learning and teaching. Review of Educational Research, 60, 1–64.

Loveless, T. (Ed.). (2001.) The great curriculum debate: How Should we teach reading and math? Brookings Institution Press, Washington, D.C.

Lubinski, C. A., Otto, A. D., Rich, B. S., & Jaberg, P. A. (1998). An analysis of two novice K-8 teachers using a model of teaching-in-context. In S. Berenson, K. Dawkins, M. Blanton, W. Coulombe, J. Kolb, K. Norwood, & L. Stiff (Eds.), Proceedings of the Twentieth Annual Meeting of the North American Chapter of the International Group for the Psychology of Mathematics Education (Vol. 2, pp. 704–709). Columbus, OH: ERIC Clearinghouse for Science, Mathematics, and Environmental Education (ERIC Document Reproduction Service No. ED 430 776).

Ma, L. (1999). Knowing and teaching elementary mathematics. Mahwah, NJ: Lawrence Erlbaum Associates.

Maher, C., & Martino, A. (1996). The development of the idea of mathematical proof: A 5-year case study. Journal for the Research of Mathematics Education, 20(1), 41–51.

McNair, R. (2000). Life outside the classroom: Implications for mathematics teaching reform. Urban Education, 34(5), 550–570.

Monk, D. H. (1994). Subject area preparation of secondary mathematics and science teachers and student achievement. Economics of Education Review, 13(2), 125–145.

Moschkovich, J. (1999). Supporting the participation of English language learners in mathematical discussions. For the Learning of Mathematics, 9(1), 11–19.

Moses, R. P., & Cobb, C. E., Jr. (2001). Radical equations: Math literacy and civil rights. Boston, MA: Beacon Press.

Mullis, I. V. S., Martin, M. O., Smith, T. A., Garden, R. A., Gregory, K. D., Gonzalez, E. J., Chrostowski, S. J., & O'Connor, K. M. (2001). TIMSS assessment frameworks and specifications 2003: IEA/TIMSS. Boston, MA: International Study Center, Lynch School of Education, Boston College (http://timss.bc.edu/timss2003i/publications.html).

Nasir, N. S. (2000). "Points ain't everything": Emergent goals and average and percent understandings in the play of basketball among African-American students. Anthropology & Education Quarterly, 31(3), 283–305.

Nasir, N. S. (2002). Identity, goals, and learning: Mathematics in cultural practice. Mathematical Thinking and Learning, 4(2/3), 213–247.

National Academy of Education. (1999). Recommendations regarding research priorities: An advisory report to the National Educational Research Policy and Priorities Board. New York, NY: National Academy of Education.

National Center for Education Statistics. (1994a). Effective schools in mathematics (NCES No. 065-000-00706-1). Washington, DC: National Center for Education Statistics Press.

National Center for Education Statistics. (1994b). A profile of the American high school sophomore in 1990 (NCES No. 95-086). Washington, DC: National Center for Education Statistics Press.

National Center for Education Statistics. (2001). The nation's report card: Mathematics 2000. Washington, DC: National Center for Education Statistics Press.

National Commission on Mathematics and Science Teaching for the 21st Century. (2000). Before it's too late. Washington, DC: U.S. Department of Education.

National Commission on Teaching and America's Future. (1996). What matters most: Teaching for America's future. New York, NY: National Commission on Teaching and America's Future.

National Council of Teachers of Mathematics. (1989). Curriculum and education standards for school mathematics. Reston, VA: National Council of Teachers of Mathematics.

National Council of Teachers of Mathematics. (2000). Principles and standards for school mathematics. Reston, VA: National Council of Teachers of Mathematics.

National Research Council, Mathematical Sciences Education Board. (1989). U.S. school mathematics from an international perspective: A guide for speakers. Washington, DC: National Research Council.

No Child Left Behind Act of 2001, Pub. L. No. 107–110, signed into law January 8, 2002 (www.ed.gov/legislation/ESEA02/).

Noss, R., Healy, L., & Hoyles, C. (1997). The construction of mathematical meanings: Connecting the visual with the symbolic. Educational Studies in Mathematics, 33, 203–233.

Noss, R., & Hoyles, C. (1996). Windows on mathematical meanings: Learning cultures and computers. Boston, MA: Kluwer Academic Publishers.

Nunes, T., Schliemann, A. D., & Carraher, D. W. (1993). Street mathematics and school mathematics. New York, NY: Cambridge University Press.

Oakes, J. (1985). Keeping Track: How schools structure inequality. New Haven, CT: Yale University Press.

Oakes, J., Gamoran, A., & Page, R. N. (1992). Curriculum differentiation: Opportunities, outcomes, and meanings. In P. W. Jackson (Ed.), Handbook of research on curriculum (pp. 570–608). New York, NY: Macmillan.

Orland, M. E. (1994). Overcoming racial barriers to equal access. In J. I. Goodlad & P. Keating (Eds.), Access to knowledge: The continuing agenda for our nations' schools. New York, NY: College Entrance Examination Board.

Owens, K. D., & Clements, M. A. (1998). Representations used in spatial problem solving in the classroom. Journal of Mathematical Behavior, 17(2), 197–218.

Paulos, J. A. (1988). Innumeracy: Mathematical illiteracy and its consequences. New York, NY: Hill and Wang.

Paulos, J. A. (1991). Beyond numeracy: Ruminations of a numbers man. New York, NY: Alfred A. Knopf.

Paulos, J. A. (1996). Mathematical illiteracy and its consequences. Speech given on the campus of Gainesville College, April 4, 1996. Gainesville, FL: Gainesville College Media Services.

Payne, K. J., & Biddle, B. J. (1999). Poor school funding, child poverty, and mathematics achievement. Educational Researcher, 28(6), 4–13.

Phillips, E., & Lappan, G. (1998). Algebra: The first gate. In L. Leutzingler (Ed.), Mathematics in the middle. Reston, VA: National Council of Teachers of Mathematics.

Ponte, J. P., Matos, J. F., Matos, J. M., & Fernandes, D. (Eds.). (1991). Mathematical problem solving and new information technologies: Research in contexts of practice (NATO ASI Series F, Vol. 89). Berlin, Germany: Springer-Verlag.

Porter, A. C., & Smithson, J. L. (2001). Are content standards being implemented in the classroom? A methodology and some tentative answers. In S. H. Fuhrman (Ed.), From the Capitol to the classroom: Standards-based reform in the states. One hundredth yearbook of the National Society for the Study of Education, Part II. Chicago, IL: University of Chicago Press.

Post, T. R., Harel, G., Behr, M. J., & Lesh, R. (1991). Intermediate teachers' knowledge of rational number concepts. In E. Fennema, T. P. Carpenter, & S. J. Lamon (Eds.), Integrating research on teaching and learning mathematics. New York, NY: State University of New York Press.

Reyes, S. A., Capella-Santana, N., & Khisty, L. L. (1998). Culturally literate teachers: Preparation for 21st century schools. In M. E. Dilworth (Ed.), Being responsive to cultural differences: How teachers learn. Thousand Oaks, CA: Corwin Press.

Rosebery, A. S., & Warren, B. (2001). Understanding diversity in science and mathematics. Hands On! 24(2), 1, 4–6.

Rothstein, E. (1995). Emblems of mind: The inner life of music and mathematics. New York, NY: Times Books/Random House.

Sabelli, N., & Dede, C. (2001). Integrating educational research and practice: Reconceptualizing goals and policies, "How to make what works work for us?" Washington, DC: National Science Foundation.

Saxe, G. B. (1991). Culture and cognitive development: Studies in mathematical understanding. Hillsdale, NJ: Lawrence Erlbaum Associates.

Saxe, G. B., Gearhart, M., & Seltzer, M. (1999). Relations between classroom practices and student learning in the domain of fractions. Cognition and Instruction, 17, 1–24.

Schifter, D. (1998). Learning mathematics for teaching: From a teachers' seminar to the classroom. Journal of Mathematics Teacher Education, 1(1), 55–87.

Schmidt, W. H., McKnight, C. C., Valverde, G. A., Houang, R. T., and Wiley, D. E. (Eds.). (1997). Many visions, many aims: A cross-national investigation of curricular intentions in school mathematics, TIMSS Volume 1, Dordrecht, Netherlands: Kluwer Academic Publishers.

Schoenfeld, A. H. (1985). Mathematical problem-solving. New York, NY: Academic Press.

Schoenfeld, A. H. (1992). Learning to think mathematically: Problem solving, metacognition, and sense making in mathematics. In D. A. Grouws (Ed.), Handbook of research on mathematics teaching and learning (pp. 334–371). New York, NY: Macmillan.

Scribner, S., & Cole, M. (1981). The psychology of literacy. Cambridge, MA: Harvard University Press.

Secada, W. G. (1990). The challenges of a changing world for mathematics education. In T. J. Cooney & C. R. Hirsch (Eds.), Teaching and learning mathematics in the 1990s: NCTM 1990 yearbook (pp. 135–143). Reston, VA: National Council of Teachers of Mathematics.

Shavelson, R. J., & Towne, L. (2002). Scientific research in education. Washington, DC: National Academy Press.

Shulman, L. (1986). Those who understand: Knowledge growth in teaching. Educational Researcher, 15, 4–14.

Shulman, L. (1987). Knowledge and teaching: Foundations of the new reform. Harvard Educational Review, 57, 1–22.

Silver, E. A., & Kenney, P. A. (Eds.). (2000). Results from the Seventh Mathematics Assessment of the National Assessment of Educational Progress. Reston, VA: National Council of Teachers of Mathematics.

Silver, E. A., & Lane, S. (1995). Can instructional reform in urban middle schools help students narrow the mathematics performance gap? Some evidence from the QUASAR Project. Research in Middle Level Education, 18(2), 49–70.

Silver, E. A., & Stein, M. K. (1996). The QUASAR project: The revolution of the possible in mathematics instructional reform in urban middle schools. Urban Education, 30(4), 476–521.

Simon, M. A. (1993). Prospective elementary teachers' knowledge of division. Journal of Research in Mathematics Education, 24(3), 233–254.

Simon, M. A., & Blume, G. W. (1994a). Building and understanding multiplicative relationships: A study of prospective elementary teachers. Journal for Research in Mathematics Education, 25(5), 472–494.

Simon, M., & Blume, G. W. (1994b). Mathematical modeling as a component of understanding ratio-as-measure: A study of prospective elementary teachers. Journal of Mathematical Behavior, 13, 183–197.

Simon, M. A., & Blume, G. W. (1996). Justification in the mathematics classroom: A study of prospective elementary teachers. Journal of Mathematical Behavior, 15(1), 3–31.

Singh, S. (1997). Fermat's enigma: The epic quest to solve the world's greatest mathematical problem. New York, NY: Anchor Books.

Smith, J. B. (1996). Does an extra year make any difference? The impact of early access to algebra in long-term gains in mathematics achievement. Educational Evaluation and Policy Analysis, 18(2), 141–153.

Steen, L. (Ed.). (2001). Mathematics and democracy: The case for quantitative literacy. Washington DC: National Council on Education and the Disciplines.

Stein, M. K., Grover, B., & Henningsen, M. (1996). Building student capacity for mathematical thinking and reasoning: An analysis of mathematical tasks used in reform classrooms. American Educational Research Journal, 33, 455–488.

Study of Instructional Improvement, Web page, The Regents of the University of Michigan, 2000 (www.sii.soe.umich.edu).

Thompson, A. G., & Thompson, P. W. (1996). Talking about rates conceptually, Part 2: Mathematical knowledge for teaching. Journal for Research in Mathematics Education, 27, 2–24.

Thompson, P. W., & Thompson, A. G. (1994). Talking about rates conceptually, Part 1: A teacher's struggle. Journal for Research in Mathematics Education, 25, 279–303.

Usiskin, Z. (Spring 1995). Why is algebra important to learn? American Educator, 19(1), 30–37.

Vergnaud, G. (1998). A comprehensive theory of representation for mathematics education. Journal of Mathematical Behavior, 17(2), 167–181.

Vershaffel, L., Greer, B., & De Corte, E. (2000). Making sense of word problems. Lisse, Netherlands: Swets & Zeitlinger.

Wagner, S. (1981). Conservation of equation and function under transformations of variable. Journal for Research in Mathematics Education, 12, 107–118.

Wheeler, D. (1996). Rough or smooth? The transition from arithmetic to algebra in problem solving. In N. Bednarz & C. Kieran (Eds.), Approaches to algebra: Perspectives for research and teaching. Dordrecht, Netherlands: Kluwer Academic Publishers.

Wheeler, M. M., & Feghali, I. (1993). Much ado about nothing: Preservice elementary teachers' conceptions of zero. Journal for Research in Mathematics Education, 24, 147–155.

Whitehead, A. N. (1962). The aims of education. London, UK: Ernest Benn.

Wilcox, S., Lanier, P., Schram, P., & Lappan, G. (1992). Influencing beginning teachers' practice in mathematics education: Confronting constraints of knowledge, beliefs, and context. Research Report 92-1. East Lansing, MI: National Center for Research on Teacher Learning, Michigan State University.

Wilensky, U. (1991). Abstract mediations on the concrete and concrete implications for mathematics education. In I. Harel & S. Papert (Eds.), Constructionism: Research reports and essays, 1985–1990 (pp. 193–204). Norwood, NJ: Ablex Publishing Corporation.

Wilson, S. M., & Berne, J. (1999). Teacher learning and the acquisition of professional knowledge: An examination of research on contemporary professional development. In A. Iran-Nejad & P. D. Pearson (Eds.). Review of research in education (Vol. 24) (pp. 173–210). Washington, DC: AERA.

Wilson, S. M., Floden, R., & Ferrini-Mundy, J. (2001). Teacher preparation research: Current knowledge, gaps, and recommendations. Seattle, WA: Center for the Study of Teaching Policy, University of Washington.

Wilson, S. M., Shulman, L. S., & Richert, A. (1987). 150 different ways of knowing: Representations of knowledge in teaching. In J. Calderhead (Ed.), Exploring teachers' thinking. Sussex, UK: Holt, Rinehart & Winston, 104–124.